# The
# Rhythm
## of the Hours

# The Rhythm
# of the Hours

## A PRAYER BOOK
## FOR EVERY DAY

# LAVINIA BYRNE

Hodder & Stoughton
LONDON SYDNEY AUCKLAND

Copyright © 2001 Lavinia Byrne

First published in Great Britain in 2001

10 9 8 7 6 5 4 3 2 1

British Library Cataloguing in Publication Data
A record for this book is available from the British Library

ISBN 0 340 75691 8

Typeset by Avon Dataset Ltd, Bidford-on-Avon, Warks

Printed and bound in Great Britain by
Clays Ltd, St Ives plc

Hodder & Stoughton
A Division of Hodder Headline Ltd
338 Euston Road
London NW1 3BH

# CONTENTS

# INTRODUCTION

At the very beginning, God created time – along with space – setting up internal rhythms and harmonies, creating night and day. And God found it very good. The very first thing that God did, according to the Book of Genesis, was to call creation into being and to give it a shape. Previously there had only been chaos, and a brooding spirit which hovered over the unformed mass. So God gave form and a pattern to light and darkness, day and night, land and sea, the animal kingdom and the plants of the earth. Our universe leapt into being.

Then God made human beings and settled us into the world he had made. The act of division, of separation, pulling dark away from light, land away from sea sounds dangerous. Yet it is matched by an act of reconciliation, for human beings are given a role within the drama of God's creative process. We are made within time and to know about time. We bring time into the divine presence by offering our time to God.

That is why, traditionally, human beings have always prayed in a patterned way, in hours and days and seasons. We offer our diligent prayer to God at regular intervals; whether we feel like praying or not, whether we experience the presence of God or not. This sacrificial, faithful prayer used to be the preserve of the Church's clergy and religious as they recite the Divine Office. These days lay people too want to pray to God within a rhythm which is not of our own creation but which mirrors the creativity of God.

Hence this book: it gives us the opportunity to give praise and thanks to God for what we have been, what we are and what we may become. For God creates and re-creates us all the time and asks us to use time to echo the marvel of our being – and that of the rest of creation – by scooping up the prayer of the universe and offering it back to God in a song or hymn of unity and praise.

On Sundays we pray with the light of the rising sun and remember the mysteries of our redemption as Christ, our life, steps out from the tomb. On Mondays, we recall the mysterious work of the Holy Spirit who calls us into being and who renews us just as the moon is renewed in the sky. On Tuesdays, we recall the love of the Father made known to us in the dayspring who comes to us from the star-filled panoply on high. Wednesdays provide a different focus for our prayer as we celebrate our earth and all that is within and upon it. Thursdays explore the theme of imagination and the gift God gives us by making us airy beings. On Friday we recall the fire that purifies and cleanses us and on Saturdays we rest in the watery hollow of the creative hand of God.

The Scriptures are full of stories about the ways in which God uses the sun and moon and stars to tell forth his praises; or the elements of earth, air, fire and water as containers for the richness of the divine message. That is why we have stories of floods and arks, bows in the sky, burning bushes, tongues of flame, spittle mixed with mud. Nothing is alien to God who is present in all things, absent from none. That is why we may safely pray from within the context of our known world to reach a God whose ultimate dwelling is beyond its present limits.

As well as the seasons of nature which are marked out for us by the place of the sun in our skies, by the onset of cold or heat, by the changing patterns of night and day, we have other rhythms too. We receive these as gifted seasons from the Church. They invite us to live a liturgical life, a life based on the contemplation of the saving mysteries of the life, death and resurrection of Christ. So Advent steals up on us as the light goes out of the sky in the northern hemisphere. Then comes Christmas, as we celebrate the birth of Jesus, followed by a festive season, keeping time with the New Year before the onset of Lent. We think about the sacred mysteries of Jesus' passion, and, with the advent of Spring, we celebrate his resurrection from the dead and keep the Easter season. At each of these holy seasons our faith is renewed and deepened; we return to the same wells, but every time we take a more refreshing and profound draught of the waters we are offered there.

Use this book at each of the moments in the Church's year; use it in your own ordinary time as well. Pray with it in the morning or evening, or both. Sing the hymns out loud or pray them silently in your heart. There are no rules. You do not have to jump through hoops or get it right. Go where the Spirit calls you and use the material you are offered here to find the God who calls you to stand upright as a beloved son or daughter of God, for this is your true destiny and your home.

Prayer is not a private possession: it is a gift, something God gives to us, something we give back to God by rejoicing in the harmony and creativity of our world. 'When you send your spirit, they are created; and you renew the face of the earth' (NIV). Those who pray with this prayer book have the desires of Psalm 104:30 at the heart of their spirituality and of their prayer.

# SUNDAY

## *Week One*

## MORNING PRAYER

### Greeting

There is in God, some say, a deep and dazzling darkness.
Henry Vaughan, 1622–95

The two tribes and the half-tribe have taken their inheritance beyond the Jordan at Jericho eastward, toward the sunrise. (Numbers 34:15)

### Reflection

Night gives way to day. As we wake up on a Sunday morning, we rise with Christ and offer praise to God. We greet the dawn and call upon the name of the Lord. The light of God dazzles us, as we seek our inheritance where the sun rises. Something is promised to us today; seize the promise. For Christ, our Lord, is risen from the dead.

### Reading

And very early on the first day of the week, when the sun had risen, they went to the tomb. They had been saying to one another, 'Who will roll away the stone for us from the entrance to the tomb?' When they looked up, they saw that the stone, which was very large, had already been rolled back. As they entered the tomb, they saw a young man, dressed in a white robe, sitting on the right side; and they were alarmed. But he said to them, 'Do not be alarmed; you are looking for Jesus of Nazareth, who was crucified. He has been raised; he is not here. Look, there is the place they laid him. But go, tell his disciples and Peter that he is going ahead of you to Galilee; there you will see him, just as he told you.' (Mark 16:2–7)

## Song

The heavens are telling the glory of God;
    and the firmament proclaims his handiwork.
Day to day pours forth speech,
    and night to night declares knowledge.
There is no speech, nor are there words;
    their voice is not heard;
yet their voice goes out through all the earth,
    and their words to the end of the world.
In the heavens he has set a tent for the sun,
which comes out like a bridegroom from his wedding canopy,
    and like a strong man runs its course with joy.
Its rising is from the end of the heavens,
    and its circuit to the end of them;
    and nothing is hid from its heat.

Psalm 19:1–9

## Prayer

Dazzling God, God of our deepest desires,
whom we meet in the night of our own doubts and our own disbelief,
as well as in the light of faith; come to us now.
Let your Holy Spirit, rising in the east, bring the daybreak to our
    hearts.
In the name of Jesus, bring us to the place of your promise, for he
    rose before us from the dead.
Grant us this with your rays, which shine to us from the heavens, Amen.

# EVENING PRAYER

## Greeting

Just when we are safest, there's a sunset-touch,
A fancy from a flower-bell, someone's death,
A chorus-ending from Euripides.

Robert Browning, 1812–89

But at the place that the Lord your God will choose as a dwelling
for his name, only there shall you offer the passover sacrifice, in
the evening at sunset, the time of day when you departed from
Egypt. (Deuteronomy 16:6)

## Reflection

In the evening, at sunset, we are reminded that every nightfall is a little death. We cast ourselves on God's care and accept the gift of freedom. As our own energy fails, we can let go of all that binds us. As night falls, we offer our prayers as an evening sacrifice and seek to live in the presence of God, as a dwelling for his name. Christ has conquered the power of darkness for he is risen from the dead.

## Reading

When it was evening on that day, the first day of the week, and the doors of the house where the disciples had met were locked for fear of the Jews, Jesus came and stood among them and said, 'Peace be with you.' After he said this, he showed them his hands and his side. Then the disciples rejoiced when they saw the Lord. Jesus said to them again, 'Peace be with you. As the Father has sent me, so I send you.' When he had said this, he breathed on them and said to them, 'Receive the Holy Spirit.' (John 20:19–22)

## Song

Abide with me; fast falls the eventide:
the darkness deepens; Lord, with me abide:
when other helpers fail, and comforts flee,
help of the helpless, O abide with me.

Swift to its close ebbs out life's little day;
earth's joys grow dim, its glories pass away;
change and decay in all around I see;
O thou who changest not, abide with me.

I need thy presence every passing hour;
what but thy grace can foil the tempter's power?
Who like thyself my guide and stay can be?
Through cloud and sunshine, Lord, abide with me.

I fear no foe, with thee at hand to bless;
ills have no weight, and tears no bitterness.
Where is death's sting? Where, grave, thy victory?
I triumph still, if thou abide with me.

Hold thou thy cross before my closing eyes;
shine through the gloom, and point me to the skies:
heaven's morning breaks, and earth's vain shadows flee;
in life, in death, O Lord, abide with me.

H. F. Lyte, 1793–1847

## Prayer

Holy Spirit, given to us on the breath of the risen Christ,
Brood over us with your warm wings.
As night falls, comfort us with your peace.
May God choose us as a dwelling for his name, Amen.

# MONDAY

## *Week One*

## MORNING PRAYER

### Greeting

For the beginning of the month is the new moon: the new moon is the new life.

St Augustine, 354–430

From new moon to new moon, and from sabbath to sabbath, all flesh shall come to worship before me, says the Lord. (Isaiah 66:23)

### Reflection

The moon, like the sun, tells us about the work of God in our world. God comes to us in the dark as well as in the light. The moon marks out time as insistently as the sun. It waxes and wanes, marking out an inner rhythm that sings to the sea and the oceans, as well as to our own working lives. As you begin a busy Monday morning, allow yourself to experience the ebb and flow of energy in your life. Go with the rhythms of the hours and do not try to stuff more into your day than it can bear.

### Reading

You have made the moon to mark the seasons; the sun knows its time for setting. You make darkness, and it is night, when all the animals of the forest come creeping out. The young lions roar for their prey, seeking their food from God. When the sun rises, they withdraw and lie down in their dens. People go out to their work and to their labour until the evening. (Psalm 104:19–23)

### Song

Through the night of doubt and sorrow
onward goes the pilgrim band,

singing songs of expectation,
marching to the promised land.

One the light of God's own presence
o'er his ransomed people shed,
chasing far the gloom and terror,
brightening all the path we tread:

One the object of our journey,
one the faith which never tires,
one the earnest looking forward,
one the hope our God inspires:

Soon shall come the great awaking,
soon the rending of the tomb;
then the scattering of all shadows,
and the end of toil and gloom.
    B. S. Ingemann, 1789–1862, tr. S. Baring-Gould, 1834–1924

## Prayer

God of the heavens, you establish the moon and the stars and set
them in place. Constellate our lives; give us purpose and direction
this day, even as we experience the ebb and flow of our own energy.
Draw us to yourself, may your Holy Spirit direct us this day and
evermore, Amen.

❧

# EVENING PRAYER

## Greeting

The moon is rightly believed to be the star of the spirit that
saturates the earth and fills bodies by its approach and empties
them by its departure. The blood even of humans increases and
diminishes with its light and leaves and herbage are sensitive to
it as the same force penetrates into all things.

Pliny, 23–79

On the day when the Lord gave the Amorites over to the
Israelites, Joshua spoke to the Lord; and he said in the sight of
Israel, 'Sun, stand still at Gibeon, and Moon, in the valley of

Aijalon.' And the sun stood still, and the moon stopped. (Joshua 10:12–13)

## Reflection

The moon is as powerful a force as the sun. It is a star of the spirit because it influences our moods and our feelings. It has its place in God's dispensation and plan. Allow God to intervene, to stop the sun and the moon if they are forcing you to adopt too fast a pace. Go with the planetary flow; let the rhythms of the sun and the moon mark out your days and nights; find God within the rhythms of nature and not apart from them.

## Reading

As they came near the village to which they were going, he walked ahead as if he were going on. But they urged him strongly, saying, 'Stay with us, because it is almost evening and the day is now nearly over.' So he went in to stay with them. When he was at the table with them, he took bread, blessed and broke it, and gave it to them. Then their eyes were opened, and they recognized him; and he vanished from their sight. (Luke 24:28–31)

## Song

The Lord whom earth and sea and sky
adore and praise and magnify,
who o'er their threefold fabric reigns,
the virgin's spotless womb contains.

And he whose will is ever done
by moon and seas, by stars and sun,
is borne upon a maiden's breast,
whom God's foreseeing grace possessed.

How blest that mother, in whose shrine
the very word of God divine,
the maker of the earth and sky,
was pleased in fleshly form to lie.

Blest in the message Gabriel brought,
blest in the work the Spirit wrought,
blest evermore, who brought to birth
the long-desired of all the earth.

O Jesu, virgin-born, to thee
eternal praise and glory be,
whom with the Father we adore
and Holy Spirit, evermore. Amen.

Tr. J. M. Neale, 1818–66

## Prayer

God, whose work in the heavens calls us to renewal and to life, grant that we may recognise you as night falls and that we may sleep safely under the glowing light of your faithful servant, the moon, Amen.

# TUESDAY
## *Week One*

## MORNING PRAYER

### Greeting

So we have the prophetic message more fully confirmed. You will do well to be attentive to this as to a lamp shining in a dark place, until the day dawns and the morning star rises in your hearts. (2 Peter 1:19)

*L'amor che muove il sole e l'altre stelle.*
True love that moves the sun and the other stars.

Dante Alighieri, 1265–1321

### Reflection

At the beginning of a new day we hear the voice of love, for the Morning Star rises in our hearts. God calls us not to fear and trembling; not to goodness or even to virtue; but to love. Whatever the past, the future begins today and brings with it the promise and possibility of renewal. Our hearts are raised in hope and praise for we are to love one another as God has loved us.

### Reading

Beloved, since God loved us so much, we also ought to love one another. No one has ever seen God; if we love one another, God lives in us, and his love is perfected in us. By this we know that we abide in him and he in us, because he has given us of his Spirit. And we have seen and do testify that the Father has sent his Son as the Saviour of the world. God abides in those who confess that Jesus is the Son of God, and they abide in God. So we have known and believe the love that God has for us. God is love, and those who abide in love abide in God, and God abides in them. Love has been perfected among us in this: that we may have boldness on the day of judgement, because as he is, so are

we in this world. There is no fear in love, but perfect love casts
out fear; for fear has to do with punishment, and whoever fears
has not reached perfection in love. We love because he first
loved us. (1 John 4:11–19)

## Song

Your steadfast love, O Lord, extends to the heavens,
   your faithfulness to the clouds.
Your righteousness is like the mighty mountains,
   your judgements are like the great deep;
   you save humans and animals alike, O Lord.
How precious is your steadfast love, O God!
   All people may take refuge in the shadow of your wings.
They feast on the abundance of your house,
   and you give them drink from the river of your delights.
For with you is the fountain of life;
   in your light we see light.
O continue your steadfast love to those who know you,
   and your salvation to the upright of heart!

Psalm 36:5–10

## Prayer

Heavenly Father, whose love extends from the heavens to earth, you
set all the stars in place and give us the life of the Morning Star,
Jesus Christ, your Son, who calls us to love you and one another
through the grace of the Holy Spirit, Amen.

♣

# EVENING PRAYER

## Greeting

Exalted manna, gladness of the best,
Heaven in ordinary, man well drest,
The Milky Way, the bird of Paradise,
Church-bells beyond the stars heard, the soul's blood,
The land of spices; something understood.

George Herbert, 1593–1633

'It is I, Jesus, who sent my angel to you with this testimony for
the churches. I am the root and the descendant of David, the
bright morning star.' (Revelation 22:16)

## Reflection

Our destiny is written in the stars because the whole of creation is caught up into God's desire to save us from what is perishable and what passes away. Each of us is made for glory; each of us is made, not simply from the earth but from the dust of the stars as well. We are marked with the sign of the promise, for the great cycle of life which is renewed by the energy of God renews us too and reminds us that we are made for heaven and that heaven is our home.

## Reading

There is one glory of the sun, and another glory of the moon, and another glory of the stars; indeed, star differs from star in glory. So it is with the resurrection of the dead. What is sown is perishable, what is raised is imperishable. It is sown in dishonour, it is raised in glory. It is sown in weakness, it is raised in power. It is sown a physical body, it is raised a spiritual body. If there is a physical body, there is also a spiritual body. Thus it is written, 'The first man, Adam, became a living being'; the last Adam became a life-giving spirit. But it is not the spiritual that is first, but the physical, and then the spiritual. The first man was from the earth, a man of dust; the second man is from heaven. As was the man of dust, so are those who are of the dust; and as is the man of heaven, so are those who are of heaven. Just as we have borne the image of the man of dust, we will also bear the image of the man of heaven. (1 Corinthians 15:41–9)

## Song

Thy kingdom come, O God,
thy rule, O Christ, begin;
break with thine iron rod
the tyrannies of sin.

Where is thy reign of peace
and purity and love?
When shall all hatred cease,
as in the realms above?

When comes the promised time
that war shall be no more,
and lust, oppression, crime
shall flee thy face before?

We pray thee, Lord, arise,
and come in thy great might;
revive our longing eyes,
which languish for thy sight.

O'er lands both near and far
thick darkness broodeth yet:
arise, O morning star,
arise, and never set!

L. Hensley, 1824–1905

## Prayer

God of all glory and hope, God whose canopy of stars hangs over us
with the promise of an imperishable destiny, help us now. The sky is
vast and we are small. Fix our gaze on the Morning Star who rises
from the dead with glory and power; open our ears to the still voice
of the Spirit who speaks as clearly in the dark as in the light; comfort
us with your love, Amen.

# WEDNESDAY
*Week One*

## MORNING PRAYER

### Greeting
To know how to live is my trade and my art.
Michel de Montaigne, 1533–92

Since we are God's offspring, we ought not to think that the deity is like gold, or silver, or stone, an image formed by the art and imagination of mortals. (Acts 17:29)

### Reflection
We have a glorious destiny, for we are made in the divine image and likeness. We are the sons and daughters of God, placed halfway between heaven and earth. So we know that God is not made in our image and likeness, nor with the tools of our trades. Rather we are made in God's image and likeness and our daily task or trade is to seek out God and to seek to live well. The earth is our dwelling place, God uses it for our salvation.

### Reading
As he walked along, [Jesus] saw a man blind from birth. His disciples asked him, 'Rabbi, who sinned, this man or his parents, that he was born blind?' Jesus answered, 'Neither this man nor his parents sinned; he was born blind so that God's works might be revealed in him. We must work the works of him who sent me while it is day; night is coming when no one can work. As long as I am in the world, I am the light of the world.' When he had said this, he spat on the ground and made mud with the saliva and spread the mud on the man's eyes, saying to him, 'Go, wash in the pool of Siloam' (which means Sent). Then he went and washed and came back able to see. (John 9:1–7)

## Song

> The earth is the Lord's and all that is in it,
>> the world, and those who live in it;
> for he has founded it on the seas,
>> and established it on the rivers.
> Who shall ascend the hill of the Lord?
>> And who shall stand in his holy place?
> Those who have clean hands and pure hearts,
>> who do not lift up their souls to what is false,
>> and do not swear deceitfully.
> They will receive blessing from the Lord,
>> and vindication from the God of their salvation.
> Such is the company of those who seek him,
>> who seek the face of the God of Jacob.

Psalm 24:1–6

## Prayer

Holy God, holy and immortal one, help us to see your face. Be the light of our world; show us your radiance shining through the dust and the mud of our present preoccupations. Keep us always mindful of those who cannot see your face and who do not know how to seek you. Set up your dwelling place within each of us and within us all, Amen.

# EVENING PRAYER

## Greeting

> O for a draught of vintage! that hath been
> Cooled a long age in the deep delvèd earth,
> Tasting of flora and the country green,
> Dance, and Provençal song, and sunburnt mirth!

John Keats, 1795–1821

Be fruitful and increase in number; fill the earth. (Genesis 1:28, NIV)

## Reflection

'The deep delvèd earth' is a place of mystery and enchantment because it is the place where God meets us and we meet God. That encounter began in a garden where God enjoyed walking with our first parents in the cool of the evening. As the prophet Micah reminds us, promise and blessing will again come to us from the earth as it puts forth fig trees and vines for our blessing and protection. So, now, as this day ends, let us risk drinking in the goodness of God who comes to us as we are and finds our companionship desirable.

## Reading

In days to come the mountain of the Lord's house shall be established as the highest of the mountains, and shall be raised up above the hills. Peoples shall stream to it, and many nations shall come and say: 'Come, let us go up to the mountain of the Lord, to the house of the God of Jacob; that he may teach us his ways and that we may walk in his paths.' For out of Zion shall go forth instruction, and the word of the Lord from Jerusalem. He shall judge between many peoples, and shall arbitrate between strong nations far away; they shall beat their swords into ploughshares, and their spears into pruning hooks; nation shall not lift up sword against nation, neither shall they learn war any more but they shall all sit under their own vines and under their own fig trees, and no one shall make them afraid; for the mouth of the Lord of hosts has spoken. (Micah 4:1–4)

## Song

Bright the vision that delighted
once the sight of Judah's seer;
sweet the countless tongues united
to entrance the prophet's ear.

Round the Lord in glory seated
cherubim and seraphim
filled his temple, and repeated
each to each the alternate hymn:

'Lord, thy glory fills the heaven;
earth is with its fullness stored;
unto thee be glory given,
holy, holy, holy, Lord.'

19

Heaven is still with glory ringing,
earth takes up the angels' cry,
'Holy, holy, holy,' singing,
'Lord of hosts, the Lord most high.'

With his seraph train before him,
with his holy Church below,
thus unite we to adore him,
bid we thus our anthem flow:

'Lord, thy glory fills the heaven;
earth is with its fullness stored;
unto thee be glory given,
holy, holy, holy, Lord.'

Richard Mant, 1776–1848

## Prayer

God of praise and might, we give you thanks for our earth, for all its
beauty and richness, for the gift of life and grace and hope. Be with
us this night and every night, in the power of your Holy Spirit and
through the gift of your Son, Jesus Christ, our Lord, Amen.

# THURSDAY

*Week One*

## MORNING PRAYER

### Greeting

The Word then is not a mere significant impression on the air,
borne by the organs of speech; nor is the Spirit of His mouth a
vapor, emitted by the organs of respiration; but the Word is He
who 'was with God in the beginning' and 'was God', and
the Spirit of the mouth of God is 'the Spirit of truth which
proceedeth from the Father'.

St Basil, b. *c.* 329

'Upon my bed this is what I saw; there was a tree at the centre
of the earth, and its height was great. The tree grew great and
strong, its top reached to heaven, and it was visible to the ends
of the whole earth. Its foliage was beautiful, its fruit abundant,
and it provided food for all. The animals of the field found shade
under it, the birds of the air nested in its branches, and from it
all living beings were fed.' (Daniel 4:10–12)

### Reflection

The Word of God is borne to us upon the air. We breathe in the
message that comes to us from God and find that it offers us freedom
and hope. For we are to be unafraid, as the kingdom of God is
growing in us. Like the birds of the air we are to move through the
world as people who trust in the generosity of our heavenly Father,
confident that we will find shelter.

### Reading

He also said, 'The kingdom of God is as if someone would scatter
seed on the ground, and would sleep and rise night and day,
and the seed would sprout and grow, he does not know how.

The earth produces of itself, first the stalk, then the head, then the full grain in the head. But when the grain is ripe, at once he goes in with his sickle, because the harvest has come.' He also said, 'With what can we compare the kingdom of God, or what parable will we use for it? It is like a mustard seed, which, when sown upon the ground, is the smallest of all the seeds on earth; yet when it is sown it grows up and becomes the greatest of all shrubs, and puts forth large branches, so that the birds of the air can make nests in its shade.' (Mark 4:26–32)

## Song

Praise the Lord!
> Happy are those who fear the Lord,
> who greatly delight in his commandments!
Their descendants will be mighty in the land;
> the generation of the upright will be blessed.
Wealth and riches are in their houses,
> and their righteousness endures forever.
They rise in the darkness as a light for the upright;
> they are gracious, merciful, and righteous.
It is well with those who deal generously and lend,
> who conduct their affairs with justice.
For the righteous will never be moved;
> they will be remembered forever.
They are not afraid of evil tidings;
> their hearts are firm, secure in the Lord.
Their hearts are steady, they will not be afraid;
> in the end they will look in triumph on their foes.
They have distributed freely, they have given to the poor;
> their righteousness endures forever;
> their horn is exalted in honour.
The wicked see it and are angry;
> they gnash their teeth and melt away;
> the desire of the wicked comes to nothing.

Psalm 112

## Prayer

Lord, make us generous, even as you are generous, Amen.

# EVENING PRAYER

## Greeting

Look at the stars! look, look up at the skies!
O look at all the fire-folk sitting in the air!
The bright boroughs, the circle-citadels there!

Gerard Manley Hopkins, 1844–89

See, I am sending my messenger to prepare the way before me,
and the Lord whom you seek will suddenly come to his temple.
The messenger of the covenant in whom you delight – indeed,
he is coming, says the Lord of hosts. (Malachi 3:1)

## Reflection

'Look at the stars', raise your eyes to the Lord. Enjoy the presence of
the Lord with all the gifts and graces that come to you when you
know that God is in the midst of you and that you are saved. Tonight,
see visions and dream dreams as your heart and your imagination
are turned to God.

## Reading

You shall know that I am in the midst of Israel, and that I, the
Lord, am your God and there is no other. And my people shall
never again be put to shame. Then afterward I will pour out my
spirit on all flesh; your sons and your daughters shall prophesy,
your old men shall dream dreams, and your young men shall
see visions. Even on the male and female slaves, in those days,
I will pour out my spirit. I will show portents in the heavens
and on the earth, blood and fire and columns of smoke. Then
everyone who calls on the name of the Lord shall be saved; for
in Mount Zion and in Jerusalem there shall be those who
escape, as the Lord has said, and among the survivors shall be
those whom the Lord calls. (Joel 2:27–32)

## Song

O worship the King all glorious above;
O gratefully sing his power and his love;
our shield and defender, the ancient of days,
pavilioned in splendour and girded with praise.

O tell of his might, O sing of his grace,
whose robe is the light, whose canopy space;
his chariots of wrath the deep thunder clouds form,
and dark is his path on the wings of the storm.

The earth with its store of wonders untold,
almighty, thy power hath founded of old;
hath 'stablished it fast by a changeless decree,
and round it hath cast, like a mantle, the sea.

Thy bountiful care what tongue can recite?
It breathes in the air, it shines in the light;
it streams from the hills, it descends to the plain,
and sweetly distils in the dew and the rain.

Frail children of dust and feeble as frail,
in thee do we trust, nor find thee to fail;
thy mercies how tender, how firm to the end!
Our maker, defender, Redeemer, and friend.

O measureless might, ineffable love,
while angels delight to hymn thee above,
thy ransomed creation, though feeble their lays,
with true adoration shall sing to thy praise.

Robert Grant, 1779–1838

## Prayer

Ancient of Days, heavenly Lord, God and Father of our Lord Jesus
Christ, visit your world this night with a vision that will bring hope
and healing for the nations, Amen.

# FRIDAY
## *Week One*

## MORNING PRAYER

### Greeting

When they had gone ashore, they saw a charcoal fire there, with fish on it, and bread. (John 21:9)

As kingfishers catch fire, dragonflies draw flame;
As tumbled over rim in roundy wells
Stones ring.

Gerard Manley Hopkins, 1844–89

### Reflection

God is revealed to Moses in the burning bush, which was consumed by fire but not destroyed. A flame of fire caught Moses' eye and he turned aside and found himself in the presence of God. God speaks to us within nature and draws us to himself so that we too may listen to him and discover his will for us. God desires to set our hearts on fire and to transform us from within.

### Reading

Moses was keeping the flock of his father-in-law Jethro, the priest of Midian; he led his flock beyond the wilderness, and came to Horeb, the mountain of God. There the angel of the Lord appeared to him in a flame of fire out of a bush; he looked, and the bush was blazing, yet it was not consumed. Then Moses said, 'I must turn aside and look at this great sight, and see why the bush is not burned up.' When the Lord saw that he had turned aside to see, God called to him out of the bush, 'Moses, Moses!' And he said, 'Here I am.' Then he said, 'Come no closer! Remove the sandals from your feet, for the place on which you are standing is holy ground.' He said further, 'I am the God of your father, the God of Abraham, the God of Isaac, and the God of Jacob.' And Moses hid his face, for he was afraid to look at God. Then the Lord said, 'I have observed the misery of my people who are in Egypt; I have heard their cry on account of their taskmasters. Indeed, I know their suffering and I have come down to deliver them from the Egyptians, and to bring them up out of that land to a good and broad land, a land flowing with milk and honey, to the country of the Canaanites, the Hittites, the Amorites, the Perizzites, the Hivites, and the Jebusites.' (Exodus 3:1–8)

## Song

O thou who camest from above,
the pure celestial fire to impart,
kindle a flame of sacred love
on the mean altar of my heart.

There let it for thy glory burn
with inextinguishable blaze,
and trembling to its source return
in humble prayer, and fervent praise.

Jesus, confirm my heart's desire
to work, and speak, and think for thee;
still let me guard the holy fire,
and still stir up thy gift in me.

Ready for all thy perfect will,
my acts of faith and love repeat,
till death thy endless mercies seal,
and make my sacrifice complete.

Charles Wesley, 1707–88

## Prayer

O God, whose pure celestial fire inflames our hearts with love, inspire us this day and every day so that we may seek and find you and burn to do your will. In the power of the Holy Spirit and the name of your beloved Son, Jesus Christ our Lord, Amen.

❧

# EVENING PRAYER

## Greeting

Whoever does not abide in me is thrown away like a branch
and withers; such branches are gathered, thrown into the fire,
and burned. (John 15:6)

So purer light shall mark the road
that leads me to the Lamb.

William Cowper, 1731–1800

## Reflection

God's fire burns, purifying and cleansing us, as well as comforting
us with its heat. We pray not to fall under judgement but to reveal
God's power to the nations and to do his will. The light of the gospel
shines upon our lives offering clarity and hope. It lights a flame in
our hearts.

## Reading

O that you would tear open the heavens and come down, so
that the mountains would quake at your presence – as when
fire kindles brushwood and the fire causes water to boil – to
make your name known to your adversaries, so that the nations
might tremble at your presence! When you did awesome deeds
that we did not expect, you came down, the mountains quaked
at your presence. From ages past no one has heard, no ear has
perceived, no eye has seen any God besides you, who works for
those who wait for him. (Isaiah 64:1–4)

## Song

It is a thing most wonderful,
almost too wonderful to be,
that God's own Son should come from heaven,
and die to save a child like me.

And yet I know that it is true:
he chose a poor and humble lot,
and wept and toiled and mourned and died
for love of those who loved him not.

I cannot tell how he could love,
a child so weak and full of sin;
his love must be most wonderful,
if he could die my love to win.

I sometimes think about the cross,
and shut my eyes, and try to see
the cruel nails and crown of thorns,
and Jesus crucified for me.

But even could I see him die,
I could but see a little part
of that great love which like a fire,
is always burning in his heart.

It is most wonderful to know
his love for me so free and sure;
but 'tis more wonderful to see
my love for him so faint and poor.

And yet I want to love thee, Lord!
O light the flame within my heart,
and I will love thee more and more,
until I see thee as thou art.

William Walsham How, 1823–97

## Prayer

Heavenly Father, light the flame of faith in our hearts so that we may not come under judgement but may do your will. Amen.

# SATURDAY

*Week One*

## MORNING PRAYER

### Greeting

The Lord is my shepherd; I shall not want. He maketh me to lie down in green pastures: he leadeth me beside the still waters. (Psalms 23:1, KJV)

I have learned
To look on nature, not as in the hour
Of thoughtless youth: but hearing oftentimes
The still, sad music of humanity.

William Wordsworth, 1770–1850

### Reflection

Water is the womb of life. The baby Moses is offered protection when he is sealed in a basket and placed in the waters of the Nile. The whole of salvation history flows from this moment, for Moses will one day open up a pathway to freedom for the Chosen People through the Red Sea. They are able to leave the slavery of Egypt and walk through the divided waters towards the Promised Land.

### Reading

Now a man from the house of Levi went and married a Levite woman. The woman conceived and bore a son; and when she saw that he was a fine baby, she hid him for three months. When she could hide him no longer she got a papyrus basket for him, and plastered it with bitumen and pitch; she put the child in it and placed it among the reeds on the bank of the river. His sister stood at a distance, to see what would happen to him. The daughter of Pharaoh came down to bathe at the river, while her attendants walked beside the river. She saw the basket among the reeds and sent her maid to bring it. When she opened it, she saw the child. He was crying, and she took pity on him, 'This must be one of the Hebrews' children,' she said. Then his sister said to Pharaoh's daughter, 'Shall I go and get you a nurse from the Hebrew women to nurse the child for you?' Pharaoh's daughter said to her, 'Yes.' So the girl went and called the child's mother. Pharaoh's daughter said to her, 'Take this child and nurse it for me, and I will give you your wages.' So the woman took the child and nursed it. When the child grew up, she brought him to Pharaoh's daughter, and she took him as her son. She named him Moses, 'because,' she said, 'I drew him out of the water.' (Exodus 2:1–10)

## Song

Jesu, lover of my soul,
let me to thy bosom fly
while the nearer waters roll,
while the tempest still is high:
hide me, O my Saviour, hide
till the storm of life is past;
safe into the haven guide,
O receive my soul at last.

Other refuge have I none,
hangs my helpless soul on thee;
leave, ah, leave me not alone,
still support and comfort me.
All my trust on thee is stayed,
all my help from thee I bring;
cover my defenceless head
with the shadow of thy wing.

Thou, O Christ, art all I want,
more than all in thee I find:
raise the fallen, cheer the faint,
heal the sick, and lead the blind.
Just and holy is thy name,
I am all unrighteousness;
false and full of sin I am,
thou art full of truth and grace.

Plenteous grace with thee is found,
grace to cover all my sin;
let the healing streams abound,
make and keep me pure within.
Thou of life the fountain art,
freely let me take of thee,
spring thou up within my heart,
rise to all eternity.

Charles Wesley, 1707–88

## Prayer

Rescue us from danger; fill our hearts with the life and joy of water;
give us your grace and call us to your service, Amen.

# EVENING PRAYER

## Greeting

Truth from the earth, like to a flow'r,
shall bud and blossom free.

John Milton, 1608–74

As the hart panteth after the water brooks, so panteth my soul
after thee, O God. (Psalm 42:1, KJV)

## Reflection

The power of God is revealed to us in the power of nature. The
presence of God in the very midst of us is revealed to us in the action
of the river that waters the Holy City of Jerusalem, making all of us
glad. Water has hidden depths; it calls us to reflect upon the need to
be silent and still, so that we can explore these depths.

## Reading

God is our refuge and strength, a very present help in trouble.
Therefore we will not fear, though the earth should change,
though the mountains shake in the heart of the sea; though its
waters roar and foam, though the mountains tremble with its
tumult. There is a river whose streams make glad the city of
God, the holy habitation of the Most High. God is in the midst
of the city; it shall not be moved; God will help it when the

morning dawns. The nations are in an uproar, the kingdoms totter; he utters his voice, the earth melts. The Lord of hosts is with us; the God of Jacob is our refuge. Come, behold the works of the Lord; see what desolations he has brought on the earth. He makes wars cease to the end of the earth; he breaks the bow, and shatters the spear; he burns the shields with fire. 'Be still, and know that I am God! I am exalted among the nations, I am exalted in the earth.' The Lord of hosts is with us; the God of Jacob is our refuge. (Psalm 46:1–11)

## Song

Father, hear the prayer we offer:
not for ease that prayer shall be,
but for strength that we may ever
live our lives courageously.

Not for ever in green pastures
do we ask our way to be;
but the steep and rugged pathway
may we tread rejoicingly.

Not for ever by still waters
would we idly rest and stay;
but would smite the living fountains
from the rocks along our way.

Be our strength in hours of weakness,
in our wanderings be our guide;
through endeavour, failure, danger,
Father, be thou at our side.

Maria Willis, 1824–1908

## Prayer

O God of power and majesty and might, be with us this night and call us to reflect upon your action in our world as we prepare for sleep, Amen.

# SUNDAY

## *Week Two*

## MORNING PRAYER

### Greeting

The mighty one, God the Lord, speaks and summons the earth from the rising of the sun to its setting. Out of Zion, the perfection of beauty, God shines forth. (Psalm 50:1–2)

This is a sovereign friendship of our courteous Lord that He keepeth us so tenderly while we be in sin; and furthermore He toucheth us full privily and sheweth us our sin by the sweet light of mercy and grace.

Julian of Norwich, *c.* 1342–1413

### Reflection

Christ is our rising sun. On the first day of the week we greet our living Saviour. We go to the tomb as the sun rises and find that the stone which hid him from our sight has been removed. We go to Galilee, to the place of encounter with the risen Lord. He greets us in love and calls us to his service. We are sent out into the world to bring the good news of our redemption to others. We see him in the full light of the sun.

### Reading

After the sabbath, as the first day of the week was dawning, Mary Magdalene and the other Mary went to see the tomb. And suddenly there was a great earthquake; for an angel of the Lord, descending from heaven, came and rolled back the stone and sat on it. His appearance was like lightning, and his clothing white as snow. For fear of him the guards shook and became like dead men. But the angel said to the women, 'Do not be afraid; I know that you are looking for Jesus who was crucified.

He is not here; for he has been raised, as he said. Come, see the place where he lay. Then go quickly and tell his disciples, "He has been raised from the dead, and indeed he is going ahead of you to Galilee; there you will see him." This is my message for you.' So they left the tomb quickly with fear and great joy, and ran to tell his disciples. Suddenly Jesus met them and said, 'Greetings!' And they came to him, took hold of his feet, and worshipped him. Then Jesus said to them, 'Do not be afraid; go and tell my brothers to go to Galilee; there they will see me.' (Matthew 28:1–10)

## Song

Awake my soul, and with the sun,
thy daily stage of duty run;
shake off dull sloth, and joyful rise
to pay thy morning sacrifice.

Redeem thy mis-spent time that's past,
live this day as if 'twere thy last:
improve thy talent with due care;
for the great day thyself prepare.

Let all thy converse be sincere,
thy conscience as the noon-day clear;
think how all-seeing God thy ways
and all thy secret thoughts surveys.

By influence of the light divine
let thy own light in good works shine;
reflect all heaven's propitious ways
in ardent love and cheerful praise.

Thomas Ken, 1637–1711

## Prayer

Loving Lord Jesus, risen from the dead, come to us now and shine the light of faith into our hearts and lives, Amen.

❧

# EVENING PRAYER

## Greeting

God called the light Day, and the darkness he called Night.
And there was evening and there was morning, the first day.
(Genesis 1:5)

Think not that the sun is brighter than He, or equal to Him: for
He who at first formed the sun must needs be incomparably
greater and brighter.

Cyril of Jerusalem, c. 376–444

## Reflection

Our faith is made strong when Jesus rises from the dead. It becomes
the cornerstone of our existence. So we realise that we are chosen
by God and that our destiny is to be a royal priesthood and a holy
nation. This Sunday evening we pray in thanksgiving as Jesus rises
from the dead and gives us light. We have been called out of
darkness; we are destined to live in the light.

## Reading

For it stands in scripture: 'See, I am laying in Zion a stone, a
cornerstone chosen and precious; and whoever believes in him
will not be put to shame.' To you then who believe, he is
precious; but for those who do not believe, 'The stone that the
builders rejected has become the very head of the corner,' and
'A stone that makes them stumble, and a rock that makes them
fall.' They stumble because they disobey the word, as they were
destined to do. But you are a chosen race, a royal priesthood, a
holy nation, God's own people, in order that you may proclaim
the mighty acts of him who called you out of darkness into his
marvellous light. Once you were not a people, but now you are
God's people; once you had not received mercy, but now you
have received mercy. (1 Peter 2:6–10)

## Song

Open to me the gates of righteousness,
that I may enter through them
and give thanks to the Lord.

This is the gate of the Lord;
>    the righteous shall enter through it.
I thank you that you have answered me
>    and have become my salvation.
The stone that the builders rejected
>    has become the chief cornerstone.
This is the Lord's doing;
>    it is marvellous in our eyes.
This is the day that the Lord has made;
>    let us rejoice and be glad in it.
Save us, we beseech you, O Lord!
>    O Lord, we beseech you, give us success!
Blessed is the one who comes in the name of the Lord.
>    We bless you from the house of the Lord.
The Lord is God,
>    and he has given us light.
Bind the festal procession with branches,
>    up to the horns of the altar.
You are my God, and I will give thanks to you;
>    you are my God, I will extol you.
O give thanks to the Lord, for he is good,
>    for his steadfast love endures forever.

Psalm 118:19–29

## Prayer

Open the eyes of faith in our hearts and minds as we greet the risen Christ. Stay with us Lord, as once you stayed with your friends. Dwell among us now and evermore, Amen.

# MONDAY

*Week Two*

## MORNING PRAYER

### Greeting

The course of the moon, and that changing which seems to the unskillful to be disorderly, is adapted to the growth of crops, and cattle, and all living creatures; for by her waxings and wanings, by a certain wonderful contrivance of providence, everything that is born is nourished and grows.

*Pseudo-Clementine Literature*, second century.

Then Moses and Aaron, Nadab, and Abihu, and seventy of the elders of Israel went up, and they saw the God of Israel. Under his feet there was something like a pavement of sapphire stone, like the very heaven for clearness. (Exodus 24:9–10)

### Reflection

The sun and the moon serve God by marking up the seasons and the rhythm of the hours. Today we reflect on the interconnectedness of all the elements in creation. All of life is here. The sun and the moon and the stars mirror back the work of God to us. We gaze into the heart of creation to see the work of the Creator and the full glory of God is disclosed to us in the rhythms of our universe.

### Reading

When I look at your heavens, the work of your fingers, the moon and the stars that you have established; what are human beings that you are mindful of them, mortals that you care for them? Yet you have made them a little lower than God, and crowned them with glory and honour. You have given them dominion over the works of your hands; you have put all things under their feet, all sheep and oxen, and also the beasts of the field, the birds of the air, and the fish of the sea, whatever passes along the paths of the seas. O Lord, our Sovereign, how majestic is your name in all the earth! (Psalm 8:3–9)

## Song

Let us, with a gladsome mind,
praise the Lord, for he is kind:
*For his mercies ay endure,*
*ever faithful, ever sure.*

Let us blaze his name abroad,
for of gods he is the God:
*For his mercies ay endure . . .*

He with all-commanding might
filled the new-made world with light:
*For his mercies ay endure . . .*

He the golden-tressed sun
caused all day his course to run:
*For his mercies ay endure . . .*

And the horned moon by night,
mid her spangled sisters bright:
*For his mercies ay endure . . .*

All things living he doth feed,
his full hand supplies their need:
*For his mercies ay endure . . .*

Let us, with a gladsome mind,
praise the Lord for he is kind:
*For his mercies ay endure . . .*

John Milton, 1608–74

## Prayer

We pray in thankfulness for the glory of God and the fullness of creation which is revealed to us within nature. Holy Spirit of all fruitfulness, come to us now, fill us with your grace, help us to know you and to praise you, Amen.

꧁

# EVENING PRAYER

## Greeting

Who is she that looketh forth as the morning, fair as the moon,
clear as the sun, and terrible as an army with banners? (Song of
Solomon 6:10, KJV)

How sweet the moonlight sleeps upon this bank!
Here will we sit, and let the sounds of music
Creep in our ears: soft stillness and the night
Become the touches of sweet harmony.

William Shakespeare, 1564–1616

## Reflection

God protects us. Even when we venture out into the wilderness,
God is there. We are carried on eagles' wings and taken to the place
of promise where the divine will is revealed to us. We are to be the
treasured possession of God who desires to bring us to a place of
safety and salvation. So the moon too marks out the time of our
salvation. Its rhythms are more complicated than those of the sun
because its shape changes as it slips in and out of the evening sky.
God is there, protecting us at all times, manifest in many different
ways.

## Reading

On the third new moon after the Israelites had gone out of the
land of Egypt, on that very day, they came into the wilderness
of Sinai. They had journeyed from Rephidim, entered the
wilderness of Sinai, and camped in the wilderness; Israel
camped there in front of the mountain. Then Moses went up to
God; the Lord called to him from the mountain, saying, 'Thus
you shall say to the house of Jacob, and tell the Israelites: You
have seen what I did to the Egyptians, and how I bore you on
eagles' wings and brought you to myself. Now therefore, if you
obey my voice and keep my covenant, you shall be my treasured
possession out of all the peoples.' (Exodus 19:1–5)

# Song

Praise the Lord! Ye heavens, adore him;
praise him, angels, in the height;
sun and moon, rejoice before him,
praise him, all ye stars and light.
Praise the Lord! For he hath spoken;
worlds his mighty voice obeyed:
laws, which never shall be broken,
for their guidance he hath made.

Praise the Lord! For he is glorious;
never shall his promise fail:
God hath made his saints victorious;
sin and death shall not prevail.
Praise the God of our salvation;
hosts on high, his power proclaim;
heaven and earth and all creation,
laud and magnify his name!

Foundling Hospital Collection, 1796

# Prayer

O God of movement and change, calling us to new life and inspiring us with hope, come to us now, strengthen us and give us your joy, Amen.

# TUESDAY
## *Week Two*

## MORNING PRAYER

### Greeting
'I see him, but not now; I behold him, but not near – a star shall come out of Jacob, and a sceptre shall rise out of Israel.' (Numbers 24:17)

My soul, there is a country
Far beyond the stars.

Henry Vaughan, 1622–95

### Reflection
The morning star rises in our hearts when we listen to the voice of the Father who says, 'This is my Son, my beloved, with whom I am well pleased.' This is a prophetic message, one that brings the light of life into our hearts and minds and makes us too into eyewitnesses of the majesty of God revealed to us in the beloved Son. We see him revealed in glory and accept that we too are made from the dust of the stars.

### Reading
We did not follow cleverly devised myths when we made known to you the power and coming of our Lord Jesus Christ, but we had been eyewitnesses of his majesty. For he received honour and glory from God the Father when that voice was conveyed to him by the Majestic Glory, saying, 'This is my Son, my Beloved, with whom I am well pleased.' We ourselves heard this voice come from heaven, while we were with him on the holy mountain. So we have the prophetic message more fully confirmed. You will do well to be attentive to this as to a lamp shining in a dark place, until the day dawns and the morning star rises in your hearts. First of all you must understand this,

that no prophecy of scripture is a matter of one's own interpretation, because no prophecy ever came by human will, but men and women moved by the Holy Spirit spoke from God. (2 Peter 1:16–21)

## Song

My God, accept my heart this day,
and make it always thine,
that I from thee no more may stray,
no more from thee decline.

Before the cross of him who died,
behold, I prostrate fall;
let every sin be crucified,
and Christ be all in all.

Anoint me with thy heavenly grace,
and seal me for thine own;
that I may see thy glorious face,
and worship near thy throne.

Let every thought and work and word
to thee be ever given:
then life shall be thy service, Lord,
and death the gate of heaven.

All glory to the Father be,
all glory to the Son,
all glory, Holy Ghost, to thee,
while endless ages run.

Matthew Bridges, 1800–94

## Prayer

Heavenly Father, you speak to us through the power of the Spirit and call us to be your eyewitnesses. Call us to your worship and praise, for Jesus' sake, Amen.

꙳

# EVENING PRAYER

## Greeting

Canst thou bind the sweet influences of Pleiades, or loose the bands of Orion? (Job 38:31, KJV)

And so, who can be found so foolish, as, when he gazes upon the fabric of the heaven, perceives the splendour of the sun and moon, sees the courses and beauty of the stars, and their paths assigned to them by fixed laws and periods, will not cry out that these things are made, not so much by a wise and rational artificer, as by wisdom and reason itself?

*Pseudo-Clementine Literature*, second century

## Reflection

A star guided the magi who came to the crib where the child Jesus lay. They put their trust in the ancient sciences of astronomy and mathematics and ventured out to find the child of the promise which they saw writ large in the sky. We pray to have some of their wisdom, to be prepared to sacrifice time and energy so that the daystar from on high may rise in our hearts too and lead us to a place where the work of God is also revealed to us.

## Reading

In the time of King Herod, after Jesus was born in Bethlehem of Judea, wise men from the East came to Jerusalem, asking, 'Where is the child who has been born king of the Jews? For we observed his star at its rising, and have come to pay him homage.' When King Herod heard this, he was frightened, and all Jerusalem with him; and calling together all the chief priests and scribes of the people, he inquired of them where the Messiah was to be born. They told him, 'In Bethlehem of Judea; for so it has been written by the prophet: "And you, Bethlehem, in the land of Judah, are by no means least among the rulers of Judah; for from you shall come a ruler who is to shepherd my people Israel."' Then Herod secretly called for the wise men and learned from them the exact time when the star had appeared. Then he sent them to Bethlehem, saying, 'Go and search diligently for the child; and when you have found him, bring me word so that I may also go and pay him homage.' When they had heard the king, they set out; and there, ahead of them, went the star that they had seen at its rising, until it stopped over the place where the child was. (Matthew 2:1–9)

## Song

As with gladness men of old
did the guiding star behold,
as with joy they hailed its light,
leading onward, beaming bright;
so, most gracious Lord, may we
evermore be led to thee.

As with joyful steps they sped,
Saviour, to thy lowly bed,
there to bend the knee before
thee whom heaven and earth adore;
so may we with willing feet
ever seek thy mercy seat.

As they offered gifts most rare
at thy cradle rude and bare,
so may we with holy joy,
pure and free from sin's alloy,
all our costliest treasures bring,
Christ, to thee our heavenly King.

Holy Jesus, every day
keep us in the narrow way,
and, when earthly things are past,
bring our ransomed souls at last
where they need no star to guide,
where no clouds thy glory hide.

In the heavenly country bright
need they no created light;
thou its light, its joy, its crown,
thou its sun which goes not down;
there forever may we sing
alleluias to our King.

W. Chatterton Dix, 1837–98

## Prayer

Guide us by your heavenly light and bring us into your presence, Lord, where we may praise you evermore, Amen.

# WEDNESDAY

## *Week Two*

## MORNING PRAYER

### Greeting

> In the beginning God created the heaven and the earth. And
> the earth was without form, and void; and darkness was upon
> the face of the deep. (Genesis 1:1–2, KJV)

> Will your anchor hold in the floods of death
> When the waters cold chill your latest breath?
> On the rising tide you can never fail,
> While your anchor holds within the veil.
>
> Priscilla Jane Owens, 1829–99

### Reflection

There is great cruelty within nature, for all new life demands and
requires the death of the old. We hand over our lives to God and to
the power of God when we go with the natural flow of life and death
as put before us by the flow of the seasons and do not try to resist
them. There is a time and a season and an hour for everything and
when we listen to the language of the earth we will learn how God
desires to direct our lives. Grace builds on nature; it does not destroy
the natural rhythms of the seasons but rather it enables us to seek
God within the patterns of our own lives and deaths.

### Reading

> Jesus answered them, 'The hour has come for the Son of Man
> to be glorified. Very truly, I tell you, unless a grain of wheat
> falls into the earth and dies, it remains just a single grain; but if
> it dies, it bears much fruit. Those who love their life lose it, and
> those who hate their life in this world will keep it for eternal
> life. Whoever serves me must follow me, and where I am, there
> will my servant be also. Whoever serves me, the Father will

honour. Now my soul is troubled. And what should I say –
"Father, save me from this hour"? No, it is for this reason that I
have come to this hour. Father, glorify your name.' Then a voice
came from heaven, 'I have glorified it, and I will glorify it again.'
(John 12:23–8)

## Song

O God of earth and altar,
Bow down and hear our cry,
Our earthly rulers falter,
Our people drift and die;
The walls of gold entomb us,
The swords of scorn divide,
Take not thy thunder from us,
But take away our pride.

From all that terror teaches,
From lies of tongue and pen,
From all the easy speeches
That comfort cruel men,
From sale and profanation
Of honour and the sword,
From sleep and from damnation,
Deliver us, good Lord!

Tie in a living tether
The prince and priest and thrall,
Bind all our lives together,
Smite us and save us all;
In ire and exultation
Aflame with faith, and free,
Lift up a living nation,
A single sword to thee.

G. K. Chesterton, 1874–1936

## Prayer

Heavenly Father, Lord of life and death, God of earth and altar,
come to us now within the rhythms of the world you have created
for us; renew us as you renew the earth, season by season and hour
by hour, and lead us to sing your praise, Amen.

❧

# EVENING PRAYER

## Greeting

Be patient, therefore, beloved, until the coming of the Lord. The farmer waits for the precious crop from the earth, being patient with it until it receives the early and the late rains. You also must be patient. Strengthen your hearts, for the coming of the Lord is near. (James 5:7–8)

Man is but earth; 'tis true; but earth is the centre. That man who dwells upon himself, who is always conversant in himself, rests in his true centre.

John Donne, 1572–1631

## Reflection

We have a spiritual destiny which calls us beyond what is presently available to us because we bear the image of the 'man of heaven', namely the Son of God. So we pray for the grace to be grounded in our own reality; to be strong and sure and secure in the knowledge that God loves us and holds us in being. We pray for the patience to persevere. The coming of the Lord is a reality for all of us, and we can hope for his coming in the certainty that we are saved.

## Reading

Listen, I will tell you a mystery! We will not all die, but we will all be changed, in a moment, in the twinkling of an eye, at the last trumpet. For the trumpet will sound, and the dead will be raised imperishable, and we will be changed. For this perishable body must put on imperishability, and this mortal body must put on immortality. When this perishable body puts on imperishability, and this mortal body puts on immortality, then the saying that is written will be fulfilled: 'Death has been swallowed up in victory.' 'Where, O death, is your victory? Where, O death, is your sting?' The sting of death is sin, and the power of sin is the law. But thanks be to God, who gives us the victory through our Lord Jesus Christ. (1 Corinthians 15:51–7)

## Song

Let all the world in every corner sing,
my God and King!
The heavens are not too high,
his praise may thither fly:
the earth is not too low,
his praises there may grow.
Let all the world in every corner sing,
my God and King!

Let all the world in every corner sing,
my God and King!
The Church with psalms must shout,
no door can keep them out;
but above all the heart
must bear the longest part.
Let all the world in every corner sing,
my God and King!

George Herbert, 1593–1632

## Prayer

My God and King, give us the grace to serve you unstintingly, and
to wait for your coming with courage and hope, Amen.

# THURSDAY
*Week Two*

## MORNING PRAYER

### Greeting
> O body swayed to music, O brightening glance,
> How can we know the dancer from the dance?
>
> W. B. Yeats, 1865–1939

> Praise him with tambourine and dance; praise him with strings
> and pipe! Praise him with clanging cymbals; praise him with
> loud clashing cymbals! Let everything that breathes praise the
> Lord! Praise the Lord! (Psalm 150:4–6)

### Reflection
'Let everything that breathes praise the Lord.' The very breath of
our bodies becomes a song and a dance of praise to the Lord when
we offer them to him. We become seasonal beings because we start
to recognise the influence of the seasons on our lives when we live
within the natural rhythms of an in-breath and an out-breath. We
become more available to God.

### Reading
> For to the one who pleases him God gives wisdom and know-
> ledge and joy; but to the sinner he gives the work of gathering
> and heaping, only to give to one who pleases God. This also is
> vanity and a chasing after wind. For everything there is a season,
> and a time for every matter under heaven: a time to be born,
> and a time to die; a time to plant, and a time to pluck up what is
> planted; a time to kill, and a time to heal; a time to break down,
> and a time to build up; a time to weep, and a time to laugh; a
> time to mourn, and a time to dance; a time to throw away stones,
> and a time to gather stones together; a time to embrace, and a
> time to refrain from embracing; a time to seek, and a time to

lose; a time to keep, and a time to throw away; a time to tear, and a time to sew; a time to keep silence, and a time to speak; a time to love, and a time to hate; a time for war, and a time for peace. (Ecclesiastes 2:26–3:8)

## Song

Come, Holy Ghost, our souls inspire,
and lighten with celestial fire;
thou the anointing Spirit art,
who dost thy sevenfold gifts impart.

Thy blessed unction from above
is comfort, life, and fire of love;
enable with perpetual light
the dullness of our blinded sight.

Anoint and cheer our soiled face
with the abundance of thy grace:
keep far our foes, give peace at home;
where thou art guide no ill can come.

Teach us to know the Father, Son,
and thee, of both, to be but one;
that through the ages all along
this may be our endless song,

'Praise to thy eternal merit,
Father, Son, and Holy Spirit.'
                    Ninth century, paraphrased by John Cosin, 1594–1672

## Prayer

'Let everything that breathes praise the Lord.' Lord God, we offer our praise to you today on every breath we breathe and in the dance of our everyday lives, Amen.

❧

# EVENING PRAYER

## Greeting

The music of the Gospel leads us home.

F. W. Faber, 1814–63

'But ask the animals, and they will teach you; the birds of the air, and they will tell you; ask the plants of the earth, and they will teach you; and the fish of the sea will declare to you. Who among all these does not know that the hand of the Lord has done this? In his hand is the life of every living thing and the breath of every human being.' (Job 12:7–10)

## Reflection

Our life is held in the hand of God who gives us breath and who holds us in being. Every breath we breathe is a gift from God and when we stop breathing, we will be caught up in the life of God so as to meet the Lord in the air. Paul writes to the people of Thessalonica to reassure them that God cares for their ultimate destiny. Those who die in Christ will be caught up into life eternal.

## Reading

But we do not want you to be uninformed, brothers and sisters, about those who have died, so that you may not grieve, as others do who have no hope. For since we believe that Jesus died and rose again, even so, through Jesus, God will bring with him those who have died. For this we declare to you by the word of the Lord, that we who are alive, who are left until the coming of the Lord, will by no means precede those who have died. For the Lord himself, with a cry of command, with the archangel's call and with the sound of God's trumpet, will descend from heaven, and the dead in Christ will rise first. Then we who are alive, who are left, will be caught up in the clouds together with them to meet the Lord in the air; and so we will be with the Lord forever. Therefore encourage one another with these words. (1 Thessalonians 4:13–18)

## Song

Hail, gladdening light, of his pure glory poured
who is the immortal Father, heavenly, blest,
holiest of holies, Jesus Christ our Lord!

Now we are come to the sun's hour of rest,
the lights of evening round us shine,
we hymn the Father, Son, and Holy Spirit divine.

Worthiest art thou at all times to be sung
with undefiled tongue,
Son of our God, giver of life, alone:
Therefore in all the world thy glories, Lord, they own.

John Keble, 1792–1866

## Prayer

As night falls, we pray for the grace to believe that we will be caught up to heaven when our ultimate destiny is revealed to us. Come, Lord, Jesus, come, Amen.

# FRIDAY
## *Week Two*

## MORNING PRAYER

### Greeting

Our faith cometh of the natural love of our soul, and of the clear light of our reason, and of the steadfast mind which we have from God in our first making.

Julian of Norwich, *c.* 1342–1413

Then the priest shall turn these into smoke on the altar as a food offering by fire for a pleasing odour. All fat is the Lord's. (Leviticus 3:16)

### Reflection

With the clear light of reason, we turn to God and realise that everything we have is held in our first making and that everything we own is ready to be given back to God. The gift of fire is about purification as we offer all that we are and everything we do back to God. With Abraham we go up the holy mountain and offer everything that is most precious to us back to God. And when we make the offering of our greatest treasures, God intervenes and gives our sacrificial gifts back to us. The fire has done its work.

### Reading

On the third day Abraham looked up and saw the place far away. Then Abraham said to his young men, 'Stay here with the donkey; the boy and I will go over there; we will worship, and then we will come back to you.' Abraham took the wood of the burnt offering and laid it on his son Isaac, and he himself carried the fire and the knife. So the two of them walked on together. Isaac said to his father Abraham, 'Father!' And he said, 'Here I am, my son.' He said, 'The fire and the wood are here, but where is the lamb for a burnt offering?' Abraham said, 'God himself will provide the lamb for a burnt offering, my son.' So the two of them walked on together. When they came to the place that God had shown him, Abraham built an altar there and laid the wood in order. He bound his son Isaac, and laid him on the altar, on top of the wood. Then Abraham reached out his hand and took the knife to kill his son. But the angel of the Lord called to him from heaven, and said, 'Abraham, Abraham!' And he said, 'Here I am.' He said, 'Do not lay your hand on the boy or do anything to him; for now I know that you fear God, since you have not withheld your son, your only son, from me.' And Abraham looked up and saw a ram, caught in a thicket by its horns. Abraham went and took the ram and offered it up as a burnt offering instead of his son. (Genesis 22:4–13)

## Song

The God of Abraham praise
who reigns enthroned above,
ancient of everlasting days,
and God of love:
Jehovah, great I AM,
by earth and heaven confest;
we bow and bless the sacred name
for ever blest.

The God of Abraham praise,
at whose supreme command
from earth we rise, and seek the joys
at his right hand:
we all on earth forsake,
its wisdom, fame, and power;
and him our only portion make,
our shield and tower.

Before the Saviour's face
the ransomed nations bow,
o'erwhelmed at his almighty grace
for ever new;
he shows his prints of love –
they kindle to a flame,
and sound through all the worlds above
the slaughtered lamb.

The whole triumphant host
give thanks to God on high;
'hail, Father, Son, and Holy Ghost,'
they ever cry;
hail! Abraham's God, and mine!
(I join the heavenly lays)
all might and majesty are thine,
and endless praise.

Thomas Olivers, 1725–99

## Prayer

Heavenly Father, in the power of your Holy Spirit, we bring our gifts to you. Receive them now in your love; purify our hearts and bless our imaginations, Amen.

# EVENING PRAYER

## Greeting

There the angel of the Lord appeared to him in a flame of fire out of a bush; he looked, and the bush was blazing, yet it was not consumed. (Exodus 3:2)

The angel of the Lord came down,
and glory shone around.

Nahum Tate, 1652–1715

## Reflection

Fire frightens us by burning with great intensity and consuming everything it touches. Yet God has always used fire as a way of speaking to us, whether in the burning bush or in the pillar of light which went ahead of the Chosen People as they made their way across the desert to find God in the Promised Land. In the new dispensation we ourselves become flames of fire, set alight with the values of the gospel, concerned to spread the light of Christ.

## Reading

Long ago God spoke to our ancestors in many and various ways by the prophets, but in these last days he has spoken to us by a Son, whom he appointed heir of all things, through whom he also created the worlds. He is the reflection of God's glory and the exact imprint of God's very being, and he sustains all things by his powerful word. When he had made purification for sins, he sat down at the right hand of the Majesty on high, having become as much superior to angels as the name he has inherited is more excellent than theirs. For to which of the angels did God ever say, 'You are my Son; today I have begotten you'? Or again, 'I will be his Father, and he will be my Son'? And again, when he brings the firstborn into the world, he says, 'Let all God's angels worship him.' Of the angels he says, 'He makes his angels winds, and his servants flames of fire.' But of the Son he says, 'Your throne, O God, is forever and ever, and the righteous sceptre is the sceptre of your kingdom.' (Hebrews 1:1–8)

## Song

And can it be that I should gain
an interest in the Saviour's blood?
Died he for me, who caused his pain;
for me, who him to death pursued?
Amazing love! – how can it be
that thou, my God, shouldst die for me?

'Tis mystery all! – the Immortal dies, –
who can explore his strange design?
In vain the first-born seraph tries
to sound the depths of love divine!
'Tis mercy all! – let earth adore,
let angel minds inquire no more.

He left his Father's throne above –
so free, so infinite his grace –
emptied himself of all but love,
and bled for Adam's helpless race.
'Tis mercy all, immense and free;
for, O my God, it found out me.

Long my imprisoned spirit lay
fast bound in sin and nature's night:
thine eye diffused a quickening ray;
I woke – the dungeon flamed with light.

My chains fell off, my heart was free;
I rose, went forth, and followed thee.

No condemnation now I dread;
Jesus, and all in him, is mine!
Alive in him, my living head,
and clothed in righteousness divine,
bold I approach the eternal throne
and claim the crown through Christ my own.

Charles Wesley, 1707–88

## Prayer
Enflame our hearts with light, so that we may become living flames
in your service, O Lord. Set us alight, Amen.

# SATURDAY
*Week Two*

## MORNING PRAYER

### Greeting
Blessed are those who trust in the Lord, whose trust is the Lord.
They shall be like a tree planted by water, sending out its roots
by the stream. It shall not fear when heat comes, and its leaves
shall stay green; in the year of drought it is not anxious, and it
does not cease to bear fruit. (Jeremiah 17:7–8)

There's a wideness in God's mercy
Like the wideness of the sea.

F. W. Faber, 1814–63

### Reflection
Jesus goes towards the Sea of Galilee and restores hearing to a deaf
man by mixing his own spittle with that of the silent supplicant. We
too turn to him now and ask for our own ears to be opened, so that
we may hear the message of the gospel in the wideness of the sea and
in the roar of living waters.

### Reading
Then he returned from the region of Tyre, and went by way of
Sidon towards the Sea of Galilee, in the region of the Decapolis.
They brought to him a deaf man who had an impediment in his
speech; and they begged him to lay his hand on him. He took
him aside in private, away from the crowd, and put his fingers
into his ears, and he spat and touched his tongue. Then looking
up to heaven, he sighed and said to him, 'Ephphatha,' that is,
'Be opened.' And immediately his ears were opened, his tongue
was released, and he spoke plainly. Then Jesus ordered them to
tell no one; but the more he ordered them, the more zealously
they proclaimed it. They were astounded beyond measure,

saying, 'He has done everything well; he even makes the deaf to hear and the mute to speak.' (Mark 7:31–7)

## Song

> Wisdom freed a holy people and a blameless race: from a nation of oppressors.
> She entered the soul of a servant of the Lord: and withstood fearsome rulers with wonders and signs.
> To the saints she gave the reward of their labours: and led them by a marvellous road.
> She was their shelter by day: and a blaze of stars by night.
> She brought them across the Red Sea: she led them through mighty waters.
> She swallowed their enemies in the waves: and spat them out from the depths of the sea.
> Then, Lord, the righteous sang the glories of your name: and praised together your protecting hand.
> For wisdom opened the mouths of the silent: and gave speech to the tongues of her children.

*Alternative Service Book*

## Prayer

Lord Jesus Christ, have mercy on me, a sinner. Lord Jesus Christ, have mercy on me, a sinner. Lord Jesus Christ, have mercy on me, a sinner, Amen.

❧

# EVENING PRAYER

## Greeting

> O God, you are my God, I seek you, my soul thirsts for you; my flesh faints for you, as in a dry and weary land where there is no water. (Psalm 63:1)

> For, though I knew His love Who followèd,
> Yet was I sore adread
> Lest, having Him, I must have naught beside.

Francis Thompson, 1859–1907

## Reflection

Our deepest thirst is our thirst for God. When Moses led the people out of Egypt into the desert, they experienced hunger and were fed with quails and manna; they also experienced thirst and needed to receive drink from the rock. With his rod, Moses struck the rock and water poured forth to sustain them. We pray for water now, for our thirst to be assuaged. We ask God to nourish and nurture us.

## Reading

From the wilderness of Sin the whole congregation of the Israelites journeyed by stages, as the Lord commanded. They camped at Rephidim, but there was no water for the people to drink. The people quarrelled with Moses, and said, 'Give us water to drink.' Moses said to them, 'Why do you quarrel with me? Why do you test the Lord?' But the people thirsted there for water; and the people complained against Moses and said, 'Why did you bring us out of Egypt, to kill us and our children and livestock with thirst?' So Moses cried out to the Lord, 'What shall I do with this people? They are almost ready to stone me.' The Lord said to Moses, 'Go on ahead of the people, and take some of the elders of Israel with you; take in your hand the staff with which you struck the Nile, and go. I will be standing there in front of you on the rock at Horeb. Strike the rock, and water will come out of it, so that the people may drink.' Moses did so, in the sight of the elders of Israel. He called the place Massah and Meribah, because the Israelites quarrelled and tested the Lord, saying, 'Is the Lord among us or not?' (Exodus 17:1–7)

## Song

Glorious things of thee are spoken,
Zion, city of our God;
he whose word cannot be broken
formed thee for his own abode.
On the rock of ages founded,
what can shake thy sure repose?
With salvation's walls surrounded,
thou mayest smile at all thy foes.

See, the streams of living waters,
springing from eternal love,
well supply thy sons and daughters,

and all fear of want remove.
Who can faint while such a river
ever flows their thirst to assuage:
grace which, like the Lord the giver,
never fails from age to age?

Round each habitation hovering,
see the cloud and fire appear
for a glory and a covering,
showing that the Lord is near.
Thus they march, the pillar leading,
light by night and shade by day;
daily on the manna feeding
which he gives them when they pray.

Saviour, since of Zion's city
I through grace a member am,
let the world deride or pity,
I will glory in thy name.
Fading is the worldling's pleasure,
all his boasted pomp and show;
solid joys and lasting treasure
none but Zion's children know.

John Newton, 1725–1807

## Prayer
Come to us, Lord, in the earthquake, wind and fire; come to us in manna and quails; come to us now, water for the life of our souls, Amen.

# SUNDAY
## *Week Three*

## MORNING PRAYER

### Greeting

The sun shall not strike you by day, nor the moon by night. The Lord will keep you from all evil; he will keep your life. (Psalm 121:6–7)

Nature is but a name for an effect,
Whose cause is God.

William Cowper, 1731–1800

### Reflection

The power of God is manifested to the prophet Job through the diversity and plenty of nature. God is the maker of all things and holds all things in being. So too with us. We are made by God and held in being as surely as the sun and the stars, the mountains and the sea. What matters is that we recognise this fact and that we give praise to God for the greatness of his deeds. In this way we will increase in our understanding of the divine purposes and grow in wisdom.

### Reading

Then Job answered: '. . . how can a mortal be just before God? If one wished to contend with him, one could not answer him once in a thousand. He is wise in heart, and mighty in strength – who has resisted him, and succeeded? – he who removes mountains, and they do not know it, when he overturns them in his anger; who shakes the earth out of its place, and its pillars tremble; who commands the sun, and it does not rise; who seals up the stars; who alone stretched out the heavens and trampled the waves of the Sea; who made the Bear and Orion, the Pleiades and the chambers of the south; who does great things

beyond understanding, and marvellous things without number.'
(Job 9:2–10)

## Song

> Christ whose glory fills the skies,
> Christ, the true, the only light,
> sun of righteousness arise,
> triumph o'er the shades of night;
> dayspring from on high, be near,
> daystar, in my heart appear.
>
> Dark and cheerless is the morn
> unaccompanied by thee;
> joyless is the day's return,
> till thy mercy's beams I see,
> till they inward light impart,
> glad my eyes, and warm my heart.
>
> Visit then this soul of mine,
> pierce the gloom of sin and grief;
> fill me, radiancy divine,
> scatter all my unbelief;
> more and more thyself display,
> shining to the perfect day.

Charles Wesley, 1707–88

## Prayer

The glory of God is made known to us in the beauty of our world.
We pray today to be strengthened in our faith. Grant us true wisdom,
Lord; help us to find you where you search for us, Amen.

# EVENING PRAYER

## Greeting

> Yours is the day, yours also the night; you established the
> luminaries and the sun. (Psalm 74:16)
>
> Now that my ladder's gone
> I must lie down where all ladders start

In the foul rag and bone shop of the heart.

W. B. Yeats, 1865–1939

## Reflection

Jacob dreams of a ladder set up between heaven and earth. He is escaping from his brother Esau's wrath, having shown that he is a cheat and a thief by stealing Esau's birthright blessing. Yet God comes to him in the watches of the night and promises him a bright future as a patriarch, a founder of a new dynasty. With the gift of the wisdom that comes to him in his dream, he discovers that the gate of heaven is opened to him. We pray for the wisdom that comes with a powerful dream. May God set a ladder in our hearts so that we join the angels and find the gate of heaven is open to us too.

## Reading

Jacob left Beer-sheba and went toward Haran. He came to a certain place and stayed there for the night, because the sun had set. Taking one of the stones of the place, he put it under his head and lay down in that place. And he dreamed that there was a ladder set up on the earth, the top of it reaching to heaven; and the angels of God were ascending and descending on it. And the Lord stood beside him and said, 'I am the Lord, the God of Abraham your father and the God of Isaac; the land on which you lie I will give to you and to your offspring; and your offspring shall be like the dust of the earth, and you shall spread abroad to the west and to the east and to the north and to the south; and all the families of the earth shall be blessed in you and in your offspring. Know that I am with you and will keep you wherever you go, and will bring you back to this land; for I will not leave you until I have done what I have promised you.' Then Jacob woke from his sleep and said, 'Surely the Lord is in this place – and I did not know it!' And he was afraid, and said, 'How awesome is this place! This is none other than the house of God, and this is the gate of heaven.' So Jacob rose early in the morning, and he took the stone that he had put under his head and set it up for a pillar and poured oil on the top of it. (Genesis 28:10–18)

## Song

O saving victim, opening wide
the gate of heaven to man below,
our foes press on from every side;
thine aid supply, thy strength bestow.

All praise and thanks to thee ascend
for evermore, blest one in three;
O grant us life that shall not end
in our true native land with thee.

St Thomas Aquinas, 1227–74, tr. J. M. Neale, 1818–66

## Prayer

Open the gate of heaven to our imaginations this night, O Lord; visit our dreams and comfort us with your presence, Amen.

# MONDAY
*Week Three*

## MORNING PRAYER

### Greeting
In his days may righteousness flourish and peace abound, until
the moon is no more. (Psalm 72:7)

Jesus shall reign where'er the sun
does his successive journeys run;
his kingdom stretch from shore to shore,
till moons shall wax and wane no more.

Isaac Watts, 1674–1748

### Reflection
Jesus is the light of our world. He is sent by the Father and comes
into our world to transform our lives. The darkness evaporates in
the presence of the light. So too with our doubts and hardness of
heart when we are exposed to the word of the Lord. Jesus does not
blame us, rather he promises us eternal life. When we listen to the
words of the light of the world, our hearts are opened, for he offers
us true life.

### Reading
Then Jesus cried aloud: 'Whoever believes in me believes not
in me but in him who sent me. And whoever sees me sees him
who sent me. I have come as light into the world, so that
everyone who believes in me should not remain in the darkness.
I do not judge anyone who hears my words and does not keep
them, for I came not to judge the world, but to save the world.
The one who rejects me and does not receive my word has a
judge; on the last day the word that I have spoken will serve as
judge, for I have not spoken on my own, but the Father who
sent me has himself given me a commandment about what to

say and what to speak. And I know that his commandment is eternal life. What I speak, therefore, I speak just as the Father has told me.' (John 12:44–50)

## Song

I heard the voice of Jesus say,
'Come unto me and rest;
lay down, thou weary one, lay down
thy head upon my breast':
I came to Jesus as I was,
weary and worn and sad;
I found in him a resting-place,
and he has made me glad.

I heard the voice of Jesus say,
'Behold I freely give
the living water, thirsty one;
stoop down and drink and live':
I came to Jesus, and I drank
of that life-giving stream;
my thirst was quenched, my soul revived,
and now I live in him.

I heard the voice of Jesus say,
'I am this dark world's light;
look unto me, thy morn shall rise,
and all thy day be bright':
I looked to Jesus, and I found
in him my star, my sun;
and in that light of life I'll walk
till travelling days are done.

Horatius Bonar, 1808–89

## Prayer

Jesus, light of our dark world, come to us now, give us the words of eternal life, Amen.

ᕑᕐ

# EVENING PRAYER

## Greeting

You have made the moon to mark the seasons; the sun knows its time for setting. (Psalm 104:19)

Was it a vision, or a waking dream?
Fled is that music: – do I wake or sleep?

John Keats, 1795–1821

## Reflection

Daniel gives thanks and praise to God because he has prayed for wisdom and God has spoken to him in the visions of the night. He grapples with the idea that God orders the world through the activity of nature and that nature mirrors the other activities of God. So he recognises the power and glory of God in the ordering of light and dark and the seasons. We pray to make the same kinds of connection, so that we too will find God mirrored back to us in the life of our world.

## Reading

Then the mystery was revealed to Daniel in a vision of the night, and Daniel blessed the God of heaven. Daniel said: 'Blessed be the name of God from age to age, for wisdom and power are his. He changes times and seasons, deposes kings and sets up kings; he gives wisdom to the wise and knowledge to those who have understanding. He reveals deep and hidden things; he knows what is in the darkness, and light dwells with him. To you, O God of my ancestors, I give thanks and praise, for you have given me wisdom and power, and have now revealed to me what we asked of you, for you have revealed to us what the king ordered.' (Daniel 2:19–23)

## Song

Light's abode, celestial Salem,
vision whence true peace doth spring,
brighter than the heart can fancy,
mansion of the highest King;

O how glorious are the praises
which of thee the prophets sing!

There for ever and for ever
alleluia is outpoured;
for unending, for unbroken
is the feast-day of the Lord;
all is pure and all is holy
that within thy walls is stored.

There no cloud or passing vapour
dims the brightness of the air;
endless noon-day, glorious noon-day,
from the sun of suns is there;
there no night brings rest from labour,
for unknown are toil and care.

O how glorious and resplendent,
fragile body, shalt thou be,
when endued with so much beauty,
full of health and strong and free,
full of vigour, full of pleasure
that shall last eternally!

Now with gladness, now with courage,
bear the burden on thee laid,
that hereafter these thy labours
may with endless gifts be paid;
and in everlasting glory
thou with brightness be arrayed.

Laud and honour to the Father,
laud and honour to the Son,
laud and honour to the Spirit,
ever three and ever one,
consubstantial, co-eternal,
while unending ages run.

Thomas à Kempis (ascribed), 1379–1471, and J. M. Neale,
1818–66

## Prayer
God of power and might, reveal your wisdom to us in the visions of this night; help us to seek and find you in all things, Amen.

# TUESDAY

*Week Three*

## MORNING PRAYER

### Greeting

Does the day-star rise?
Still thy stars do fall and fall.
Does day close his eyes?
Still the fountain weeps for all.
Let night or day do what they will,
Thou hast thy task; thou weepest still.

Richard Crashaw, *c.* 1613–49

'It is I, Jesus, who sent my angel to you with this testimony for the churches. I am the root and the descendant of David, the bright morning star.' (Revelation 22:16)

### Reflection

God seeks to be a wall of fire around us and to dwell in the midst of us, to be a powerful presence in our world and our lives. God is energetic, purposeful, a warrior, who intervenes on behalf of his Chosen People. We pray now for the protection which we are promised as we face a complicated world which seeks to exclude him and does not want the wall of fire of God's power, seeking its own glory apart from him and not within him.

### Reading

'For I will be a wall of fire all around it, says the Lord, and I will be the glory within it.' Up, up! Flee from the land of the north, says the Lord; for I have spread you abroad like the four winds of heaven, says the Lord. Up! Escape to Zion, you that live with daughter Babylon. For thus said the Lord of hosts (after his glory sent me) regarding the nations that plundered you: Truly, one who touches you touches the apple of my eye. See now, I am going to raise my hand against them, and they shall become plunder for their own slaves. Then you will know that the Lord of hosts has sent me. Sing and rejoice, O daughter Zion! For lo, I will come and dwell in your midst, says the Lord. Many nations shall join themselves to the Lord on that day, and shall be my people; and I will dwell in your midst. And you shall know that the Lord of hosts has sent me to you. The Lord will inherit Judah as his portion in the holy land, and will again choose Jerusalem. (Zechariah 2:5–12)

## Song

All hail the power of Jesu's name;
let angels prostrate fall;
bring forth the royal diadem
to crown him Lord of all.

Crown him, ye morning stars of light,
who fixed this floating ball;
now hail the strength of Israel's might,
and crown him Lord of all.

Crown him, ye martyrs of your God,
who from his altar call;
praise him whose way of pain ye trod,
and crown him Lord of all.

Ye seed of Israel's chosen race,
ye ransomed of the fall,
hail him who saves you by his grace,
and crown him Lord of all.

Hail him, ye heirs of David's line,
whom David Lord did call;
the God incarnate, man divine,
and crown him Lord of all.

Sinners, whose love can ne'er forget
the wormwood and the gall,
go spread your trophies at his feet,
and crown him Lord of all.

Let every tribe and every tongue
to him their hearts enthral,
lift high the universal song
and crown him Lord of all.

Edward Perronet, 1726–92, and John Rippon, 1751–1836

## Prayer

We pray to the Lord of all, the wall of fire who protects our lives.
Open our hearts, come and dwell in the midst of us, receive our
prayers, Amen.

❧

# EVENING PRAYER

## Greeting

But the slow watches of the night
not less to God belong;
and for the everlasting right
the silent stars are strong.

Frederick Lucian Hosmer, 1840–1929

'Remember Abraham, Isaac, and Israel, your servants, how you
swore to them by your own self, saying to them, "I will multiply
your descendants like the stars of heaven, and all this land that
I have promised I will give to your descendants, and they shall
inherit it forever." ' (Exodus 32:13)

## Reflection

God asks Abram to look up at the sky and to count the stars. They
are of course, uncountable, especially when you view them in the
black and silent darkness of a desert night. Gradually your eyes
come into focus as you gaze on a vision of infinity. That was the
nature of the promise God made to the father of Isaac and of all the
future generations of his people. They are to be infinite in number.
Abraham is our father in the faith. We share in the promise revealed
to him in the stars that glowed in the desert sky.

## Reading

After these things the word of the Lord came to Abram in a
vision, 'Do not be afraid, Abram, I am your shield; your reward

shall be very great.' But Abram said, 'O Lord GOD, what will you give me, for I continue childless, and the heir of my house is Eliezer of Damascus?' And Abram said, 'You have given me no offspring, and so a slave born in my house is to be my heir.' But the word of the Lord came to him, 'This man shall not be your heir; no one but your very own issue shall be your heir.' He brought him outside and said, 'Look toward heaven and count the stars, if you are able to count them.' Then he said to him, 'So shall your descendants be.' And he believed the Lord; and the Lord reckoned it to him as righteousness. (Genesis 15:1–6)

## Song

Who are these, like stars appearing,
these before God's throne who stand?
Each a golden crown is wearing;
who are all this glorious band?
Alleluya, hark! they sing,
praising loud their heavenly King.

Who are these of dazzling brightness,
these in God's own truth arrayed,
clad in robes of purest whiteness,
robes whose lustre ne'er shall fade,
ne'er be touched by time's rude hand –
whence comes all this glorious band?

These are they who have contended
for their Saviour's honour long,
wrestling on till life was ended,
following not the sinful throng;
these, who well the fight sustained,
triumph through the lamb have gained.

These are they whose hearts were riven,
sore with woe and anguish tried,
who in prayer full oft have striven
with the God they glorified;
now, their painful conflict o'er,
God has bid them weep no more.

These like priests have watched and waited,
offering up to Christ their will,
soul and body consecrated,
day and night to serve him still:
now, in God's most holy place
blest they stand before his face.

H. T. Schenck, 1656–1727, tr. Frances E. Fox, 1812–97

## Prayer

We gaze at the stars and contemplate our spiritual destiny. Lord God, father of Abraham and of us all, illumine us with a vision of hope for our own future, Amen.

# WEDNESDAY

*Week Three*

## MORNING PRAYER

### Greeting

'He humbled you by letting you hunger, then by feeding you with manna, with which neither you nor your ancestors were acquainted, in order to make you understand that one does not live by bread alone, but by every word that comes from the mouth of the Lord.' (Deuteronomy 8:3)

Batter my heart, three-personed God; for, you
As yet but knock, breathe, shine, and seek to mend.

John Donne, 1572–1631

### Reflection

The word of God is not something remote or mysterious or alien. The Book of Deuteronomy reassures us that the word is 'very near'. The gift of life is given to us, incarnated in the person of Jesus who speaks God into our midst. We are called to attend to the word of God which is available to us here – now.

### Reading

For the Lord will again take delight in prospering you, just as he delighted in prospering your ancestors, when you obey the Lord your God by observing his commandments and decrees that are written in this book of the law, because you turn to the Lord your God with all your heart and with all your soul. Surely, this commandment that I am commanding you today is not too hard for you, nor is it too far away. It is not in heaven, that you should say, 'Who will go up to heaven for us, and get it for us so that we may hear it and observe it?' Neither is it beyond the sea, that you should say, 'Who will cross to the other side of the sea for us, and get it for us so that we may

hear it and observe it?' No, the word is very near to you;
it is in your mouth and in your heart for you to observe.
(Deuteronomy 30:9–14)

## Song

All my hope on God is founded;
he doth still my trust renew.
Me through change and chance he guideth,
only good and only true.
God unknown,
he alone
calls my heart to be his own.

Pride of man and earthly glory,
sword and crown betray his trust;
what with care and toil he buildeth,
tower and temple, fall to dust.
But God's power,
hour by hour,
is my temple and my tower.

God's great goodness aye endureth,
deep his wisdom, passing thought:
splendour, light, and life attend him,
beauty springeth out of naught.
Evermore
from his store
new-born worlds rise and adore.

Daily doth th'Almighty Giver
bounteous gifts on us bestow;
his desire our soul delighteth,
pleasure leads us where we go.
Love doth stand
at his hand;
joy doth wait on his command.

Still from man to God eternal
sacrifice of praise be done,
high above all praises praising
for the gift of Christ his Son.

Christ doth call
one and all
ye who follow shall not fall.

Robert Bridges, 1844–1930

## Prayer

Source of our hope, source of our joy, come, Lord Jesus, come. Speak your word into our hearts and into our mouths. Be near to us, Amen.

❧

# EVENING PRAYER

## Greeting

And all this brought our Lord suddenly to my mind, and shewed these words, and said: I am Ground of thy beseeching: first it is my will that thou have it; and after, I make thee to will it; and after, I make thee to beseech it and thou beseechest it. How should it then be that thou shouldst not have thy beseeching?

Julian of Norwich, c.1342–1413

Boaz the father of Obed by Ruth, and Obed the father of Jesse, and Jesse the father of King David. (Matthew 1:5)

## Reflection

Boaz's generosity to Ruth mirrors her generosity to her mother-in-law, Naomi. This is one of the most tender stories in the Bible. It shows God's loving concern for his people for Boaz will marry Ruth and her grandchild will be King David. The land will be secure. For God knows our need to be grounded and rooted, to have a home, a place where we belong. With Ruth and Naomi, we journey to our own Bethlehem, confident that God will give us the earth as our inheritance.

## Reading

Then Boaz said to Ruth, 'Now listen, my daughter, do not go to glean in another field or leave this one, but keep close to my young women. Keep your eyes on the field that is being reaped, and follow behind them. I have ordered the young men not to bother you. If you get thirsty, go to the vessels and drink from what the young men have drawn.' Then she fell prostrate, with her face to the ground, and said to him, 'Why have I found favour in your sight, that you should take notice of me, when I am a foreigner?' But Boaz answered her, 'All that you have done for your mother-in-law since the death of your husband has been fully told me, and how you left your father and mother and your native land and came to a people that you did not know before. May the Lord reward you for your deeds, and may you have a full reward from the Lord, the God of Israel, under whose wings you have come for refuge!' Then she said, 'May I continue to find favour in your sight, my lord, for you have comforted me and spoken kindly to your servant, even though I am not one of your servants.' At mealtime Boaz said to her, 'Come here, and eat some of this bread, and dip your morsel in the sour wine.' So she sat beside the reapers, and he heaped up for her some parched grain. She ate until she was satisfied, and she had some left over. When she got up to glean, Boaz instructed his young men, 'Let her glean even among the standing sheaves, and do not reproach her. You must also pull out some handfuls for her from the bundles, and leave them for her to glean, and do not rebuke her.' So she gleaned in the field until evening. Then she beat out what she had gleaned, and it was about an ephah of barley. (Ruth 2:8–17)

## Song

Lord, enthroned in heavenly splendour,
first-begotten from the dead,
thou alone, our strong defender,
liftest up thy people's head.
Alleluia!
Jesu, true and living bread.

Here our humblest homage pay we,
here in loving reverence bow;
here for faith's discernment pray we,
lest we fail to know thee now.
Alleluia!
Thou art here, we ask not how.

Though the lowliest form doth veil thee
as of old in Bethlehem,

here as there thine angels hail thee,
branch and flower of Jesse's stem.
Alleluia!
We in worship join with them.

Paschal lamb, thine offering, finished
once for all when thou wast slain,
in its fullness undiminished
shall for evermore remain.
Alleluia!
Cleansing souls from every stain.

Life-imparting heavenly manna,
stricken rock with streaming side,
heaven and earth with loud hosanna
worship thee, the lamb who died.
Alleluia!
Risen, ascended, glorified!

G. H. Bourne, 1840–1925

## Prayer

Lord God, Ground of our being, bring us to truth, to life and to hope; bring us to Bethlehem, where we may meet you in the simple kindness of our friends, and in the gift of bread, Amen.

# THURSDAY

*Week Three*

## MORNING PRAYER

### Greeting

'The wind blows where it chooses, and you hear the sound of it, but you do not know where it comes from or where it goes. So it is with everyone who is born of the Spirit.' (John 3:8)

To all swift things for swiftness did I sue;
Clung to the whistling mane of every wind.

Francis Thompson, 1859–1907

### Reflection

The gift of the Holy Spirit is given with the sound of a rush of violent wind and with tongues of flame. God speaks to us in the mystery of the work of the wind, now gently, now in a tornado for it blows where it chooses and swirls around our planet swirling us all into a vision of life. We live on the wind for it is what we breathe and as much our life force as is food or drink. Today we ask to be strengthened with the gifts of the Holy Spirit as the apostles were and we sing St Francis' great canticle in praise of all the elements of creation.

### Reading

When the day of Pentecost had come, they were all together in one place. And suddenly from heaven there came a sound like the rush of a violent wind, and it filled the entire house where they were sitting. Divided tongues, as of fire, appeared among them, and a tongue rested on each of them. All of them were filled with the Holy Spirit and began to speak in other languages, as the Spirit gave them ability. Now there were devout Jews from every nation under heaven living in Jerusalem. And at this sound the crowd gathered and was bewildered, because each one heard them speaking in the native language of each.

Amazed and astonished, they asked, 'Are not all these who are
speaking Galileans? And how is it that we hear, each of us, in
our own native language?' (Acts 2:1–8)

## Song

All creatures of our God and King,
lift up your voice and with us sing
alleluia, alleluia!
Thou burning sun with golden beam,
thou silver moon with softer gleam,
*O praise him, O praise him,*
*Alleluia, alleluia, alleluia!*

Thou rushing wind that art so strong,
ye clouds that sail in heaven along,
O praise him, alleluia!
Thou rising morn, in praise rejoice,
ye lights of evening, find a voice;
*O praise him, O praise him . . .*

Thou flowing water, pure and clear,
make music for thy Lord to hear,
alleluia, alleluia!
Thou fire so masterful and bright,
that givest man both warmth and light,
*O praise him, O praise him . . .*

Dear mother earth, who day by day
unfoldest blessings on our way,
O praise him, alleluia!
The flowers and fruits that in thee grow,
let them his glory also show;
*O praise him, O praise him . . .*

Let all things their creator bless,
and worship him in humbleness;
O praise him, alleluia!
Praise, praise the Father, praise the Son,
and praise the Spirit, three in One;
*O praise him, O praise him . . .*

W. H. Draper, 1855–1933, based on St Francis, 1182–1226

## Prayer

Blow into our lives, Holy Spirit of God. Encourage us to renew our faith, hope and charity for the praise and service of your holy name, Amen.

❧

# EVENING PRAYER

## Greeting

'Take no gold, or silver, or copper in your belts, no bag for your journey, or two tunics, or sandals, or a staff; for labourers deserve their food.' (Matthew 10:9–10)

Does the road wind up-hill all the way?
Yes, to the very end.
Will the day's journey take the whole long day?
From morn to night, my friend.

Christina Rossetti, 1830–94

## Reflection

Paul has been arrested. He is to be taken to Rome. The wind goes against the progress of the soldiers' boat and all hope of being saved has to be abandoned. We pray to understand the traumas we go through, recognising that nature speaks to us of our tragedies as well as our joys. Every journey tests our faith for we meet with obstacles as well as blessings. Today we pray for the courage that supported Paul in his service of the gospel.

## Reading

When a moderate south wind began to blow, they thought they could achieve their purpose; so they weighed anchor and began to sail past Crete, close to the shore. But soon a violent wind, called the northeaster, rushed down from Crete. Since the ship was caught and could not be turned head-on into the wind, we gave way to it and were driven. By running under the lee of a small island called Cauda we were scarcely able to get the ship's boat under control. After hoisting it up they took measures to undergird the ship; then, fearing that they would run on the Syrtis, they lowered the sea anchor and so were driven. We were being pounded by the storm so violently that on the next day they began to throw the cargo overboard, and on the third day with their own hands they threw the ship's tackle overboard. When neither sun nor stars appeared for many days, and no small tempest raged, all hope of our being saved was at last abandoned. (Acts 27:13–20)

## Song

Who would true valour see,
let him come hither;
one here will constant be,
come wind, come weather;
there's no discouragement
shall make him once relent
his first avowed intent
to be a pilgrim.

Whoso beset him round
with dismal stories,
do but themselves confound;
his strength the more is.
No lion can him fright;
he'll with a giant fight,
but he will have the right
to be a pilgrim.

No goblin nor foul fiend
can daunt his spirit;
he knows he at the end
shall life inherit.
Then, fancies, fly away;
he'll fear not what men say;
he'll labour night and day
to be a pilgrim.

John Bunyan, 1628–88

## Prayer

Lord Jesus Christ, give us the valour to follow you faithfully and to seek your will at all times, even when adversity knocks the wind out of our sails and we are tempted to despair, Amen.

# FRIDAY
## *Week Three*

## MORNING PRAYER

### Greeting

You make the winds your messengers, fire and flame your ministers. (Psalm 104:4)

Breathe on me, breath of God,
till I am wholly thine;
until this earthly part of me
glows with thy fire divine.

Edwin Hatch, 1835–89

### Reflection

God uses fire to pour out his grace upon us. He gives the gifts of the Spirit so that we can encounter danger without fear. For God alone can take away our anxieties and give us the strength to go out and proclaim his glory. Each of the images of Scripture feeds upon another as the authors of the sacred text turn again and again to their experience of the elements and of God's work within creation to teach his word and explain his saving deeds.

### Reading

But now thus says the Lord, he who created you, O Jacob, he who formed you, O Israel: Do not fear, for I have redeemed you; I have called you by name, you are mine. When you pass through the waters, I will be with you; and through the rivers, they shall not overwhelm you; when you walk through fire you shall not be burned, and the flame shall not consume you. For I am the Lord your God, the Holy One of Israel, your Saviour. I give Egypt as your ransom, Ethiopia and Seba in exchange for you. Because you are precious in my sight, and honoured, and I love you, I give people in return for you, nations in

exchange for your life. Do not fear, for I am with you; I will
bring your offspring from the east, and from the west I will
gather you; I will say to the north, 'Give them up,' and to the
south, 'Do not withhold; bring my sons from far away and my
daughters from the end of the earth – everyone who is called by
my name, whom I created for my glory, whom I formed and
made.' (Isaiah 43:1–7)

## Song

Sun, who all my life dost brighten,
light, who dost my soul enlighten,
joy, the sweetest man e'er knoweth,
fount, whence all my being floweth,
at thy feet I cry, my maker,
let me be a fit partaker
of this blessed food from heaven,
for our good, thy glory, given.

Jesus, bread of life, I pray thee,
let me gladly here obey thee;
never to my hurt invited,
be thy love with love requited:
from this banquet let me measure,
Lord, how vast and deep its treasure;
through the gifts thou here dost give me
as thy guest in heaven receive me.
Johann Franck, 1618–77, tr. Catherine Winkworth, 1827–78

## Prayer

All-powerful God, pour out your Holy Spirit upon us so that we can
lay down our fears and persevere in our service of your holy word,
Amen.

# EVENING PRAYER

## Greeting

Big fires flare up in a wind, but little ones are blown out unless
they are carried in under cover.

Francis de Sales, 1567–1622

As [Elisha and Elijah] continued walking and talking, a chariot of fire and horses of fire separated the two of them, and Elijah ascended in a whirlwind into heaven. (2 Kings 2:11)

## Reflection

Fire is tricky stuff. Elijah used it in his ministry when he destroyed the prophets of the false god, Baal. At the end of his life God came to him in a chariot of fire. Yet at his time of greatest trial and spiritual growth Elijah found God in a totally different and unexpected encounter. Not in the earthquake, wind and fire that were so familiar to him, but rather in the still, small voice. We pray to listen to God in the stillness and ask for his silent word to breathe into our own lives.

## Reading

[Elijah] got up, and ate and drank; then he went in the strength of that food forty days and forty nights to Horeb the mount of God. At that place he came to a cave, and spent the night there. Then the word of the Lord came to him, saying, 'What are you doing here, Elijah?' He answered, 'I have been very zealous for the Lord, the God of hosts; for the Israelites have forsaken your covenant, thrown down your altars, and killed your prophets with the sword. I alone am left, and they are seeking my life, to take it away.' He said, 'Go out and stand on the mountain before the Lord, for the Lord is about to pass by.' Now there was a great wind, so strong that it was splitting mountains and breaking rocks in pieces before the Lord, but the Lord was not in the wind; and after the wind an earthquake, but the Lord was not in the earthquake; and after the earthquake a fire, but the Lord was not in the fire; and after the fire a sound of sheer silence. When Elijah heard it, he wrapped his face in his mantle and went out and stood at the entrance of the cave. Then there came a voice to him that said, 'What are you doing here, Elijah?' (1 Kings 19:8–13)

## Song

Dear Lord and Father of mankind,
forgive our foolish ways;
reclothe us in our rightful mind;
in purer lives thy service find,
in deeper reverence, praise.

In simple trust like their who heard,
beside the Syrian sea,
the gracious calling of the Lord,
let us, like them, without a word
rise up and follow thee.

O Sabbath rest by Galilee!
O calm of hills above,
where Jesus knelt to share with thee
the silence of eternity,
interpreted by love!

Drop thy still dews of quietness,
till all our strivings cease;
take from our souls the strain and stress,
and let our ordered lives confess
the beauty of thy peace.

Breathe through the heats of our desire
thy coolness and thy balm;
let sense be dumb, let flesh retire;
speak through the earthquake, wind and fire,
O still small voice of calm.

John Greenleaf Whittier, 1807–92

## Prayer
Grant us the grace to listen to you now. Come to us in the earthquake, wind and fire. Come to us in the still, small voice, Amen.

# SATURDAY
## *Week Three*

## MORNING PRAYER

### Greeting

> When the earth and all its people quake, it is I who hold its pillars firm. (Psalm 75:3, NIV)
>
> Nearer and nearer draws the time,
> the time that shall surely be,
> when the earth shall be filled with the glory of God
> as the waters cover the sea.
>
> Arthur Ainger, 1841–1919

### Reflection

God protects his people by day with a pillar of cloud and at night with a pillar of fire. Inexorably their journey brings them to the sea, the place of encounter with their fears. We reflect on all the mysteries that we associate with water: the flood and covenant of the rainbow, the passage across the Dead Sea, the baptism of Jesus, our own baptism. Each of these mingles fear with mercy. We pray now for an experience of the mercy of God. God is transcendent, immortal, invisible, yet manifest to us in the mysteries of our faith.

### Reading

> They set out from Succoth, and camped at Etham, on the edge of the wilderness. The Lord went in front of them in a pillar of cloud by day, to lead them along the way, and in a pillar of fire by night, to give them light, so that they might travel by day and by night. Neither the pillar of cloud by day nor the pillar of fire by night left its place in front of the people. Then the Lord said to Moses: Tell the Israelites to turn back and camp in front of Pi-hahiroth, between Migdol and the sea, in front of Baal-zephon; you shall camp opposite it, by the sea. (Exodus 13:20–14:2)

## Song

Immortal, invisible, God only wise,
in light inaccessible hid from our eyes,
most blessed, most glorious, the ancient of days,
almighty, victorious, thy great name we praise.

Unresting, unhasting, and silent as light,
nor wanting, nor wasting, thou rulest in might;
thy justice like mountains high soaring above
thy clouds which are fountains of goodness and love.

To all life thou givest, to both great and small;
in all life thou livest, the true life of all;
we blossom and flourish as leaves on the tree,
and wither and perish; but naught changeth thee.

Great Father of glory, pure Father of light,
thine angels adore thee, all veiling their sight;
all laud we would render: O help us to see
'tis only the splendour of light hideth thee.

W. Chalmers Smith, 1824–1908

## Prayer

Pillar of cloud, pillar of fire, loving God, bring us to the water of
eternal life, Amen.

# EVENING PRAYER

## Greeting

You trampled the sea with your horses, churning the mighty
waters. (Habakkuk 3:15)

The vast unmeasurable sea, gathered together by His working
into various basins, never passes beyond the bounds placed
around it, but does as He has commanded.

Clement of Rome, *c.* 96

## Reflection

The sea is an image of all that is most uncontrollable and most unknown in our universe. Its life is hidden from us because its true depths are so unknown. When we go to sea we experience the raw power of the waves and the immensity of its scope, compared with our own frail and fragile lives. To control the sea is to exercise power on a scale that defies human imagination. In this gospel story, we witness the fear of the disciples as they face danger and then their sense of bafflement when Jesus shows his power over the waves.

## Reading

One day he got into a boat with his disciples, and he said to them, 'Let us go across to the other side of the lake.' So they put out, and while they were sailing he fell asleep. A gale swept down on the lake, and the boat was filling with water, and they were in danger. They went to him and woke him up, shouting, 'Master, Master, we are perishing!' And he woke up and rebuked the wind and the raging waves; they ceased, and there was a calm. He said to them, 'Where is your faith?' They were afraid and amazed, and said to one another, 'Who then is this, that he commands even the winds and the water, and they obey him?' (Luke 8:22–5)

## Song

Eternal Father, strong to save,
whose arm doth bind the restless wave,
who bidd'st the mighty ocean deep
its own appointed limits keep;
O hear us when we cry to thee
for those in peril on the sea.

O Saviour, whose almighty word
the winds and waves submissive heard,
who walkedst on the foaming deep,
and calm amid its rage didst sleep:
O hear us when we cry to thee
for those in peril on the sea.

O sacred Spirit, who didst brood
upon the chaos dark and rude,
who bad'st its angry tumult cease,

and gavest light and life and peace:
O hear us when we cry to thee
for those in peril on the sea.

O Trinity of love and power,
our brethren shield in danger's hour;
from rock and tempest, fire and foe,
protect them whereso'er they go:
and ever let there rise to thee
glad hymns of praise from land and sea.

William Whiting, 1825–78

## Prayer

Come to us now, Lord Jesus Christ. Travel with us as we face the waves that threaten to harm us and to overwhelm our frail lives. Command the winds and the waves and show us your majesty, Amen.

# SUNDAY
*Week Four*

## MORNING PRAYER

### Greeting
May his name endure forever, his fame continue as long as the sun. May all nations be blessed in him; may they pronounce him happy. (Psalm 72:17)

Life-imparting heavenly manna,
stricken rock with streaming side,
heaven and earth with loud hosanna
worship thee, the lamb who died,
Alleluia!
Risen, ascended, glorified!

George Hugh Bourne, 1840–1925

### Reflection
God provides manna from heaven. The sun rises each morning and dries the layer of dew that greets the Israelites as they open their tent flaps and continue their journey into the wilderness. They receive quails at nightfall and with the new dawn a new experience, bread from heaven, manna from on high. In this way, the glory of the Lord is revealed within nature. The rising sun becomes a sign of hope and sustenance for our own journey of faith. It promises us life and the renewal of life.

### Reading
In the evening quails came up and covered the camp; and in the morning there was a layer of dew around the camp. When the layer of dew lifted, there on the surface of the wilderness was a fine flaky substance, as fine as frost on the ground. When the Israelites saw it, they said to one another, 'What is it?' For they did not know what it was. Moses said to them, 'It is the bread

that the Lord has given you to eat. This is what the Lord has commanded: "Gather as much of it as each of you needs, an omer to a person according to the number of persons, all providing for those in their own tents." ' The Israelites did so, some gathering more, some less. But when they measured it with an omer, those who gathered much had nothing over, and those who gathered little had no shortage; they gathered as much as each of them needed. And Moses said to them, 'Let no one leave any of it over until morning.' But they did not listen to Moses; some left part of it until morning, and it bred worms and became foul. And Moses was angry with them. Morning by morning they gathered it, as much as each needed; but when the sun grew hot, it melted. (Exodus 16:13–21)

## Song

How sweet the name of Jesus sounds
in a believer's ear!
It soothes his sorrows, heals his wounds,
and drives away his fear.

It makes the wounded spirit whole,
and calms the troubled breast;
'tis manna to the hungry soul,
and to the weary rest.

Dear name! the rock on which I build,
my shield and hiding-place,
my never ending treasury filled
with boundless stores of grace.

Jesus! my shepherd, brother, friend,
my prophet, priest, and King,
my Lord, my life, my way, my end,
accept the praise I bring.

Weak is the effort of my heart,
and cold my warmest thought;
but when I see thee as thou art,
I'll praise thee as I ought.

Till then would I thy love proclaim
with every fleeting breath;
and may the music of thy name
refresh my soul in death.

John Newton, 1725–1807

## Prayer

Give us your manna today, Lord God. Feed us as once you fed your chosen people. Sustain us with your hope as the sun rises and we rejoice because we celebrate your Son's resurrection from the dead, Amen.

❧

# EVENING PRAYER

## Greeting

Remember your creator in the days of your youth, before the days of trouble come, and the years draw near when you will say, 'I have no pleasure in them'; before the sun and the light and the moon and the stars are darkened and the clouds return with the rain. (Ecclesiastes 12:1–2)

I give you the end of a golden string;
Only wind it into a ball:
It will lead you in at Heaven's gate,
Built in Jerusalem's wall.

William Blake, 1757–1827

## Reflection

Jerusalem the golden reflects the light of heaven back to us. The author of the Book of Revelation describes a vision in which he is transported beyond our present world. He fixes our attention on the light of the lamp which is the Lamb. Heaven and earth, as we understand them, may pass away but the glory of the Lord remains forever. This vision of Jerusalem is not about earthly reality but about the destiny which lies ahead of us, beyond the final sleep of death. At that moment true brilliance will be revealed and the sun becomes dispensable, its rays redundant as we journey forward into the new life which awaits us beyond the grave.

## Reading

And in the spirit he carried me away to a great, high mountain and showed me the holy city Jerusalem coming down out of heaven from God. It has the glory of God and a radiance like a very rare jewel, like jasper, clear as crystal . . . The wall is built of jasper, while the city is pure gold, clear as glass. The foundations of the wall of the city are adorned with every jewel; the first was jasper, the second sapphire, the third agate, the fourth emerald, the fifth onyx, the sixth cornelian, the seventh chrysolite, the eighth beryl, the ninth topaz, the tenth chrysoprase, the eleventh jacinth, the twelfth amethyst. And the twelve gates are twelve pearls, each of the gates is a single pearl, and the street of the city is pure gold, transparent as glass. I saw no temple in the city, for its temple is the Lord God the Almighty and the Lamb. And the city has no need of sun or moon to shine on it, for the glory of God is its light, and its lamp is the Lamb. The nations will walk by its light, and the kings of the earth will bring their glory into it. (Revelation 21:10–11, 18–24)

## Song

Jerusalem the golden,
with milk and honey blest,
beneath thy contemplation
sink heart and voice opprest.
I know not, O I know not,
what social joys are there,
what radiancy of glory,
what light beyond compare.

They stand, those halls of Sion,
conjubilant with song,
and bright with many an angel,
and all the martyr throng;
the Prince is ever in them,
the daylight is serene,
the pastures of the blessed
are decked in glorious sheen.

There is the throne of David,
and there, from care released,
the song of them that triumph,

the shout of them that feast;
and they who, with their leader,
have conquered in the fight,
for ever and for ever
are clad in robes of white.

O sweet and blessed country,
shall I ever see thy face?
O sweet and blessed country,
shall I ever win thy grace?
Exult, O dust and ashes!
The Lord shall be thy part:
his only, his for ever,
thou shalt be, and thou art.

Bernard of Cluny, twelfth century, tr. J. M. Neale, 1818–66

## Prayer

Lord Jesus Christ, Lamb of God, light of our world and of future glory, shine into our hearts tonight. Give us the grace to know you now and to seek you in the life to come, Amen.

*next*

# MONDAY
## *Week Four*

## MORNING PRAYER

### Greeting

By heaven methinks it were an easy leap
To pluck bright honour from the pale-faced moon.

William Shakespeare, 1564–1616

May he live while the sun endures, and as long as the moon, throughout all generations. (Psalms 72:5)

### Reflection

Like Nicodemus, we come to Jesus by night. We sit with him and listen to his teaching. We are reminded that 'no one can see the kingdom of God without being born from above'. We pray to understand what 'above' means. We lift our eyes to the heavens and gaze into space, seeking to understand worlds which lie beyond our own. We pray to have a wider and a broader vision, one which takes us beyond what is presently known to us. The gentle light of the moon shines on our searching.

### Reading

Now there was a Pharisee named Nicodemus, a leader of the Jews. He came to Jesus by night and said to him, 'Rabbi, we know that you are a teacher who has come from God; for no one can do these signs that you do apart from the presence of God.' Jesus answered him, 'Very truly, I tell you, no one can see the kingdom of God without being born from above.' Nicodemus said to him, 'How can anyone be born after having grown old? Can one enter a second time into the mother's womb and be born?' Jesus answered, 'Very truly, I tell you, no one can enter the kingdom of God without being born of water and Spirit. What is born of the flesh is flesh, and what is born of the

Spirit is spirit. Do not be astonished that I said to you, "You must be born from above." The wind blows where it chooses, and you hear the sound of it, but you do not know where it comes from or where it goes. So it is with everyone who is born of the Spirit.' (John 3:1–8)

## Song

The maker of the sun and moon,
The maker of our earth,
Lo, late in time, a fairer boon,
Himself is brought to birth.

How blest was all creation then,
When God so gave increase;
And Christ, to heal the hearts of men,
Brought righteousness and peace.

His human form, by man denied,
Took death for human sin;
His endless love, through faith descried,
Still lives the world to win.

O perfect love, outpassing sight,
O light beyond our ken,
Come down through all the world tonight,
And heal the hearts of men!

Laurence Housman, 1865–1959

## Prayer

Heavenly Father, shine down on our searching; heal our hearts and minds; heal the wounds of our world, Amen.

# EVENING PRAYER

## Greeting

Blow the trumpet at the new moon, at the full moon, on our festal day. For it is a statute for Israel, an ordinance of the God of Jacob. (Psalm 81:3–4)

My flesh in hope shall rest,
and for a season slumber:
till trump from east to west
shall wake the dead in number.

George Ratcliffe Woodward, 1848–1934

## Reflection

God stands in judgement over us. Do we use our time wisely? Are we simply concerned to exploit the moment and the people of the moment, or are we concerned to mirror the generosity of God by being generous ourselves? It is not simply we who are to be 'ransomed, healed, restored, forgiven', our world too requires redemption. The attitudes and values of the gospel must so permeate our lives that the whole world is transformed and enjoys a sweet rather than a bitter day.

## Reading

This what the Lord God showed me: a basket of summer fruit. He said, 'Amos, what do you see?' And I said, 'A basket of summer fruit.' Then the Lord said to me, 'The end has come upon my people Israel; I will never again pass them by. The songs of the temple shall become wailings on that day,' says the Lord God; 'the dead bodies shall be many, cast out in every place. Be silent!' Hear this, you that trample on the needy, and bring to ruin the poor of the land, saying, 'When will the new moon be over so that we may sell grain; and the sabbath, so that we may offer wheat for sale? We will make the ephah small and the shekel great, and practise deceit with false balances, buying the poor for silver and the needy for a pair of sandals, and selling the sweepings of the wheat' . . . On that day, says the Lord God, I will make the sun go down at noon, and darken the earth in broad daylight. I will turn your feasts into mourning, and all your songs into lamentation; I will bring sackcloth on all loins, and baldness on every head; I will make it like the mourning for an only son, and the end of it like a bitter day. (Amos 8:1–6, 9–10)

## Song

Praise, my soul, the King of heaven;
to his feet thy tribute bring.
Ransomed, healed, restored, forgiven,

who like me his praise should sing?
Praise him! Praise him!
Praise the everlasting King.

Praise him for his grace and favour
to our fathers in distress;
praise him still the same for ever,
slow to chide, and swift to bless.
Praise him! Praise him!
Glorious in his faithfulness.

Father-like, he tends and spares us;
well our feeble frame he knows;
in his hands he gently bears us,
rescues us from all our foes.
Praise him! Praise him!
Widely as his mercy flows.

Angels, help us to adore him;
ye behold him face to face;
sun and moon, bow down before him;
dwellers all in time and space.
Praise him! Praise him!
Praise with us the God of grace.

H. F. Lyte, 1793–1847

## Prayer

Lord God of grace, source of all life, transform our hearts so that we use our time to serve you and not to exploit others and their rights, open our minds to reflect on the concerns of our world, Amen.

# TUESDAY
## *Week Four*

## MORNING PRAYER

### Greeting

'To the one who conquers I will also give the morning star.'
(Revelation 2:28)

Christian! seek not yet repose,
Hear thy guardian angel say;
Thou art in the midst of foes.

Charlotte Elliott, 1789–1871

### Reflection

As the stars of the morning rise in our hearts, we reflect on the
works of darkness and on the armour of light. Where do dark and
light lie for us today? How can we aspire to live in the light? For like
the angels, we are called to praise God by living within the dispensation of grace. This is the kingdom of heaven, the kingdom of God,
where love reigns supreme.

### Reading

Love does no wrong to a neighbour; therefore, love is the
fulfilling of the law. Besides this, you know what time it is, how
it is now the moment for you to wake from sleep. For salvation
is nearer to us now than when we became believers; the night is
far gone, the day is near. Let us then lay aside the works of
darkness and put on the armour of light; let us live honourably
as in the day, not in revelling and drunkenness, not in debauch-
ery and licentiousness, not in quarrelling and jealousy. Instead,
put on the Lord Jesus Christ, and make no provision for the
flesh, to gratify its desires. (Romans 13:10–14)

## Song

> Stars of the morning, so gloriously bright,
> filled with celestial resplendence and light,
> these that, where night never followeth day,
> raise the trisagion ever and ay:
>
> These are thy counsellors, these dost thou own,
> Lord God of Sabaoth, nearest thy throne;
> these are thy ministers, these dost thou send,
> help of the helpless ones! Man to defend.
>
> These keep the guard amid Salem's dear bowers;
> thrones, principalities, virtues, and powers;
> where, with the living ones, mystical four,
> cherubim, seraphim bow and adore.
>
> 'Who like the Lord?' thunders Michael the chief;
> Raphael, 'the cure of God', comforteth grief;
> and, as at Nazareth, prophet of peace,
> Gabriel, 'the light of God', bringeth release.
>
> Then, when the earth was first poised in mid space,
> then, when the planets first sped on their race,
> then, when were ended the six days' employ,
> then all the sons of God shouted for joy.
>
> Still let them succour us; still let them fight,
> Lord of angelic hosts, battling for right;
> till, where their anthems they ceaselessly pour,
> we with the angels may bow and adore.
>
> St Joseph the Hymnographer, d. 883, tr. J. M. Neale,
> 1818–66

## Prayer

With the holy angels and archangels, we sing unceasing praises to God, saying, 'Holy, holy, holy Lord God of hosts, fill our hearts with love and true kindness, this day and ever more. Call us to live in the light, Amen.

༄

# EVENING PRAYER

## Greeting

Sun and moon shall darkened be,
Stars shall fall, the heav'ns shall flee.

Christopher Wordsworth, 1807–85

Moses said to him, 'As soon as I have gone out of the city, I will
stretch out my hands to the Lord; the thunder will cease, and
there will be no more hail, so that you may know that the earth
is the Lord's.' (Exodus 9:29)

## Reflection

God speaks fierce words of condemnation to the people through the
mouth of the prophet, Ezekiel. Our stars will be made dark and the
moon will not yield up her light when we fail to fulfil the word of the
Lord and neglect the commandments of God. Nature is cast into
disarray by human sin. For everything in creation is a vehicle of
God's grace to us; nothing is excluded from his care or from his
power. We are mistaken if we think that God is not concerned about
our world. We too have a duty of care towards it as well as towards
each other.

## Reading

Thus says the Lord GOD: In an assembly of many peoples I will
throw my net over you; and I will haul you up in my dragnet. I
will throw you on the ground, on the open field I will fling you,
and will cause all the birds of the air to settle on you, and I will
let the wild animals of the whole earth gorge themselves on
you. I will strew your flesh on the mountains, and fill the valleys
with your carcass. I will drench the land with your flowing
blood up to the mountains, and the watercourses will be filled
with you. When I blot you out, I will cover the heavens, and
make their stars dark; I will cover the sun with a cloud, and the
moon shall not give its light. All the shining lights of the heavens
I will darken above you, and put darkness on your land, says
the Lord GOD. (Ezekiel 32:3–8)

## Song

> Praise the Lord!
> Praise the Lord from the heavens;
>> praise him in the heights!
> Praise him, all his angels;
>> praise him, all his host!
> Praise him, sun and moon;
>> praise him, all you shining stars!
> Praise him, you highest heavens,
>> and you waters above the heavens!
> Let them praise the name of the Lord,
>> for he commanded and they were created.
> He established them for ever and ever;
>> he fixed their bounds, which cannot be passed.
> Praise the Lord from the earth,
>> you sea monsters and all deeps,
> fire and hail, snow and frost,
>> stormy wind fulfilling his command!
> Mountains and all hills,
>> fruit trees and all cedars!
> Wild animals and all cattle,
>> creeping things and flying birds!
> Kings of the earth and all peoples,
>> princes and all rulers of the earth!
> Young men and women alike,
>> old and young together!
> Let them praise the name of the Lord,
>> for his name alone is exalted;
>> his glory is above earth and heaven.
> He has raised up a horn for his people,
>> praise for all his faithful,
>> for the people of Israel who are close to him.
> Praise the Lord!

Psalm 148:1–14

## Prayer

Lord God of all creation, we pray with the whole of creation and offer you thanks for the beauty of a universe where every star has its place, and all is gift and all is grace, Amen.

# WEDNESDAY

## *Week Four*

## MORNING PRAYER

### Greeting

The earth is the Lord's and all that is in it, the world, and those who live in it. (Psalm 24:1)

Nature that framed us of four elements,
Warring within our breasts for regiment,
Doth teach us all to have aspiring minds:
Our souls, whose faculties can comprehend
The wondrous architecture of the world.

Christopher Marlowe, 1564–93

### Reflection

Moses sends spies ahead of the people to investigate the land of promise. On their return, they describe the fruit and vegetables that they have seen in the land that flows with milk and honey and, as well, they bring a single cluster of grapes, supported on a pole. With pomegranates and figs, this is living proof that God intends to bless them through the fruit of the earth and the work of their hands. They touch evidence of the 'wondrous architecture of the world'.

### Reading

And they came to the Wadi Eshcol, and cut down from there a branch with a single cluster of grapes, and they carried it on a pole between two of them. They also brought some pomegranates and figs. That place was called the Wadi Eshcol, because of the cluster that the Israelites cut down from there. At the end of forty days they returned from spying out the land. And they came to Moses and Aaron and to all the congregation of the Israelites in the wilderness of Paran, at Kadesh; they brought back word to them and to all the congregation, and showed them the fruit of the land. And they told him, 'We came to the land to which you sent us; it flows with milk and honey, and this is its fruit.' (Numbers 13:23–7)

## Song

O God, our help in ages past,
our hope for years to come,
our shelter from the stormy blast,
and our eternal home;

beneath the shadow of thy throne
thy saints have dwelt secure;
sufficient is thine arm alone,
and our defence is sure.

Before the hills in order stood,
or earth received her frame,
from everlasting thou art God,
to endless years the same.

A thousand ages in thy sight
are like an evening gone,
short as the watch that ends the night
before the rising sun.

Time, like an ever-rolling stream,
bears all its sons away;
they fly forgotten, as a dream
dies at the opening day.

O God, our help in ages past,
our hope for years to come,
be thou our guard while troubles last,
and our eternal home.

Isaac Watts, 1674–1748

## Prayer

God of heaven and earth, bless us through the fruits of the earth; bless our hearts and our imaginations as we contemplate the order of the hills and the frame of the earth, Amen.

꽃

# EVENING PRAYER

## Greeting

Let me sing for my beloved my love-song concerning his vineyard: My beloved had a vineyard on a very fertile hill. (Isaiah 5:1)

Every man shall eat in safety
Under his own vine what he plants; and sing
The merry songs of peace to all his neighbours.

William Shakespeare, 1564–1616

## Reflection

The earth is rich with the promise of God and Jesus is the true vine who grows at the heart of it. Fruitfulness is a sign of God's blessing and so is peace, for if we are ourselves part of the vine, then we abide in the Father and God's will is made known to others through the lives we lead. We are not to be miserable or miserly. Rather we are to be bountiful and to lead lives which give glory to God.

## Reading

'I am the true vine, and my Father is the vine-grower. He removes every branch in me that bears no fruit. Every branch that bears fruit he prunes to make it bear more fruit. You have already been cleansed by the word that I have spoken to you. Abide in me as I abide in you. Just as the branch cannot bear fruit by itself unless it abides in the vine, neither can you unless you abide in me. I am the vine, you are the branches. Those who abide in me and I in them bear much fruit, because apart from me you can do nothing. Whoever does not abide in me is thrown away like a branch and withers; such branches are gathered, thrown into the fire, and burned. If you abide in me, and my words abide in you, ask for whatever you wish, and it will be done for you. My Father is glorified by this, that you bear much fruit and become my disciples. As the Father has loved me, so I have loved you; abide in my love.' (John 15:1–9)

## Song

Bread of heaven, on thee we feed,
for thy flesh is meat indeed;
ever may our souls be fed
with this true and living bread;
day by day with strength supplied
through the life of him who died.

Vine of heaven, thy blood supplies
this blest cup of sacrifice;
Lord, thy wounds our healing give,
to thy cross we look and live:
Jesus, may we ever be
grafted, rooted, built in thee.

Josiah Conder, 1789–1855

## Prayer

Vine of heaven, vine of earth, call us to abide in your love. Make us generous in your service, Amen.

# THURSDAY

*Week Four*

## MORNING PRAYER

### Greeting

Cherish pity, lest you drive an angel from your door.
William Blake, 1757–1827

The angel of the Lord called to him from heaven, and said,
'Abraham, Abraham!' And he said, 'Here I am.' (Genesis 22:11)

### Reflection

The air is full of airy beings. Angels fly between us and God, spirit
beings who are concerned to fulfil the Lord's commands. The angel
who brings a scroll to the author of the Book of Revelation, like the
angel who brings the news of the promise to Mary at the Annuncia-
tion, is a bearer of the word of God, able to seal up the contrary
voices which oppose the will of God and to open and disclose the
divine purpose. The word of God is directed to all of us and each of
us must receive it and consume it and be consumed by it.

### Reading

And I saw another mighty angel coming down from heaven,
wrapped in a cloud, with a rainbow over his head; his face was
like the sun, and his legs like pillars of fire. He held a little
scroll open in his hand. Setting his right foot on the sea and his
left foot on the land, he gave a great shout, like a lion roaring.
And when he shouted, the seven thunders sounded. And when
the seven thunders had sounded, I was about to write, but I
heard a voice from heaven saying, 'Seal up what the seven
thunders have said, and do not write it down.' Then the angel
whom I saw standing on the sea and the land raised his right
hand to heaven and swore by him who lives forever and ever,
who created heaven and what is in it, the earth and what is in it,

and the sea and what is in it: 'There will be no more delay, but in the days when the seventh angel is to blow his trumpet, the mystery of God will be fulfilled, as he announced to his servants the prophets.' Then the voice that I had heard from heaven spoke to me again, saying, 'Go, take the scroll that is open in the hand of the angel who is standing on the sea and on the land.' So I went to the angel and told him to give me the little scroll; and he said to me, 'Take it, and eat; it will be bitter to your stomach, but sweet as honey in your mouth.' (Revelation 10:1–9)

## Song

Ye holy angels bright,
who wait at God's right hand,
or through the realms of light
fly at your Lord's command,
assist our song,
for else the theme
too high doth seem
for mortal tongue.

Ye blessed souls at rest,
who ran this earthly race,
and now, from sin released,
behold the Saviour's face,
his praises sound,
as in his light
with sweet delight
ye do abound.

Ye saints who toil below,
adore your heavenly King,
and onward as ye go
some joyful anthem sing;
take what he gives
and praise him still,
through good and ill,
who ever lives.

My soul, bear thou thy part,
triumph in God above,

and with a well-tuned heart
sing thou the songs of love.
Let all thy days
till life shall end
whate'er he send,
be filled with praise.

Richard Baxter, 1615–91

## Prayer

'Heaven and earth are full of your glory.' Heavenly Lord, God of
earth and sky and sea, come to us now, take away our fear and
deliver your word into the midst of us, Amen.

❧

# EVENING PRAYER

## Greeting

'My God sent his angel and shut the lions' mouths so that they
would not hurt me, because I was found blameless before him.'
(Daniel 6:22)

Grant us thy peace, Lord, through the coming night;
turn thou for us its darkness into light.

John Elterton, 1826–93

## Reflection

When Jesus had finished his Last Supper with the apostles, he went
out onto the Mount of Olives. As he prayed to fulfil God's will, an
angel from heaven gave him strength. The worlds of heaven and
earth meet when we turn to God in time of trial and need. We pray
tonight to the Blessed Trinity, thanking God for the great work of
our redemption and for the intervention of the angels in
communicating the will of God to us.

## Reading

He came out and went, as was his custom, to the Mount of
Olives; and the disciples followed him. When he reached the
place, he said to them, 'Pray that you may not come into the
time of trial.' Then he withdrew from them about a stone's throw,
knelt down, and prayed, 'Father, if you are willing, remove this

cup from me; yet, not my will but yours be done.' Then an angel from heaven appeared to him and gave him strength. In his anguish he prayed more earnestly, and his sweat became like great drops of blood falling down on the ground. When he got up from prayer, he came to the disciples and found them sleeping because of grief, and he said to them, 'Why are you sleeping? Get up and pray that you may not come into the time of trial.' (Luke 22:39–46)

## Song

Father most holy, merciful and loving,
Jesu, Redeemer, ever to be worshipped,
life-giving Spirit, comforter most gracious,
God everlasting.

Three in a wondrous unity unbroken,
one perfect Godhead, love that never faileth,
light of the angels, succour of the needy,
hope of all living;

All thy creation serveth its creator,
thee every creature praiseth without ceasing;
we too would sing thee psalms of true devotion:
hear, we beseech thee.

Lord God almighty, unto thee be glory,
one in three persons, over all exalted.
Thine, as is meet, be honour, praise and blessing
now and for ever.

                    Tenth century, tr. Alfred Edward Alston, 1862–1927

## Prayer

'Not mine but thy will be done.' We pray tonight for all those who are struggling and in pain. We pray for prisoners and refugees, for the poor, the sick and the lonely. We pray for ourselves, Amen.

# FRIDAY

*Week Four*

## MORNING PRAYER

### Greeting

Now if anyone builds on the foundation with gold, silver, precious stones, wood, hay, straw – the work of each builder will become visible, for the Day will disclose it, because it will be revealed with fire, and the fire will test what sort of work each has done. (1 Corinthians 3:12–13)

And that a higher gift than grace
should flesh and blood refine
God's presence and his very self,
and essence all divine.

John Henry Newman, 1801–90

### Reflection

God's fire sets us alight with zeal; it strengthens our faith by illuminating our imaginations. It sets our hearts alight. But there is also another dimension to the fire of God, for it judges and refines us by testing us. Only precious stones and metals can withstand the full blast of its power. God's fire asks us to explore our lives and to evaluate them ourselves so that we prepare for the day of judgement by anticipating its effects. God's fire cuts and divides as well, sorting out our true allegiances.

### Reading

'I came to bring fire to the earth, and how I wish it were already kindled! I have a baptism with which to be baptized, and what stress I am under until it is completed! Do you think that I have come to bring peace to the earth? No, I tell you, but rather division! From now on five in one household will be divided, three against two and two against three; they will be divided:

father against son and son against father, mother against daughter and daughter against mother, mother-in-law against her daughter-in-law and daughter-in-law against mother-in-law.' He also said to the crowds, 'When you see a cloud rising in the west, you immediately say, "It is going to rain"; and so it happens. And when you see the south wind blowing, you say, "There will be scorching heat"; and it happens. You hypocrites! You know how to interpret the appearance of earth and sky, but why do you not know how to interpret the present time? And why do you not judge for yourselves what is right?' (Luke 12:49–57)

## Song

Judge eternal, throned in splendour,
Lord of lords and King of kings,
with thy living fire of judgement
purge this realm of bitter things:
solace all its wide dominion
with the healing of thy wings.

Still the weary folk are pining
for the hour that brings release:
and the city's crowded clangour
cries aloud for sin to cease;
and the homesteads and the woodlands
plead in silence for their peace.

Crown, O God, thine own endeavour:
cleave our darkness with thy sword:
feed the faint and hungry heathen
with the richness of thy word:
cleanse the body of this empire
through the glory of the Lord.

Henry Scott Holland, 1847–1918

## Prayer

Fire of God, power of God, cleanse our hearts and imaginations with your light. Loving Judge, set us free, Amen.

✣

# EVENING PRAYER

## Greeting

God said, 'This is the sign of the covenant that I make between
me and you and every living creature that is with you, for all
future generations: I have set my bow in the clouds, and it shall
be a sign of the covenant between me and the earth.' (Genesis
9:12–13)

To you all angels, all the powers of heaven,
    cherubim and seraphim sing in endless praise:
Holy, holy, holy Lord, God of power and might,
    heaven and earth are full of your glory.

*Te Deum*

## Reflection

Solomon brings together all the elders of the people to receive the
ark of the covenant with the tablets of the law as it is taken to the
new temple which he has built as a house for the Lord. The cherubim
protect it and the priests commit themselves to God's service. Then
God comes to dwell in the midst of his people revealing himself in
the cloud of glory. The fire of God's glory shines around us now as
we consecrate our hearts to be a place where God may dwell and be
revealed.

## Reading

Then Solomon assembled the elders of Israel and all the heads
of the tribes, the leaders of the ancestral houses of the Israelites,
before King Solomon in Jerusalem, to bring up the ark of the
covenant of the Lord out of the city of David, which is Zion . . .
Then the priests brought the ark of the covenant of the Lord to
its place, in the inner sanctuary of the house, in the most holy
place, underneath the wings of the cherubim. For the cherubim
spread out their wings over the place of the ark, so that the
cherubim made a covering above the ark and its poles. There
was nothing in the ark except the two tablets of stone that Moses
had placed there at Horeb, where the Lord made a covenant
with the Israelites, when they came out of the land of Egypt.
And when the priests came out of the holy place, a cloud filled

the house of the Lord, so that the priests could not stand to minister because of the cloud; for the glory of the Lord filled the house of the Lord. Then Solomon said, 'The Lord has said that he would dwell in thick darkness. I have built you an exalted house, a place for you to dwell in forever.' (1 Kings 8:1, 6–13)

## Song

Holy, holy, holy! Lord God almighty!
Early in the morning our song shall rise to thee;
holy, holy, holy! merciful and mighty!
God in three persons, blessed Trinity!

Holy, holy, holy! all the saints adore thee,
casting down their golden crowns around the glassy sea;
cherubim and seraphim falling down before thee,
which wert and art and evermore shall be.

Holy, holy, holy! though the darkness hide thee,
though the eye of sinful man thy glory may not see,
only thou art holy, there is none beside thee
perfect in power, in love, and purity.

Holy, holy, holy! Lord God almighty!
All thy works shall praise thy name in earth and sky and sea;
holy, holy, holy! merciful and mighty!
God in three persons, blessed Trinity.

Reginald Heber, 1783–1826

## Prayer

Holy Lord God, come to us now, dwell in us in your true holiness.
Make us holy, Amen.

# SATURDAY

*Week Four*

## MORNING PRAYER

### Greeting

But he answered them, 'An evil and adulterous generation asks
for a sign, but no sign will be given to it except the sign of the
prophet Jonah. For just as Jonah was three days and three
nights in the belly of the sea monster, so for three days and
three nights the Son of Man will be in the heart of the earth.'
(Matthew 12:39–40)

I must go down to the sea again, to the vagrant gypsy life,
To the gull's way and the whale's way where the wind's like a
    whetted knife.

John Masefield, 1878–1967

### Reflection

The prophet Jonah is an unlikely candidate for God's call. He tries
to run away from it, escaping by sea. But God's plan and God's call
prevail and Jonah is thrown overboard by nervous sailors. A great
sea fish descends upon him and swallows him up. He praises God
from within the belly of the whale, singing of the divine power God
exercises over the waters of the sea and the mysteries of the deep.
His three days there prefigure the three days that Jesus will spend
in the sealed tomb.

### Reading

So they picked Jonah up and threw him into the sea; and the
sea ceased from its raging. Then the men feared the Lord even
more, and they offered a sacrifice to the Lord and made vows.
But the Lord provided a large fish to swallow up Jonah; and
Jonah was in the belly of the fish for three days and three
nights. Then Jonah prayed to the Lord his God from the belly

of the fish, saying, 'I called to the Lord out of my distress, and he answered me; out of the belly of Sheol I cried, and you heard my voice. You cast me into the deep, into the heart of the seas, and the flood surrounded me; all your waves and your billows passed over me. Then I said, "I am driven away from your sight; how shall I look again upon your holy temple?" The waters closed in over me; the deep surrounded me; weeds were wrapped around my head at the roots of the mountains. I went down to the land whose bars closed upon me forever; yet you brought up my life from the Pit, O Lord my God. As my life was ebbing away, I remembered the Lord; and my prayer came to you, into your holy temple. Those who worship vain idols forsake their true loyalty. But I with the voice of thanksgiving will sacrifice to you; what I have vowed I will pay. Deliverance belongs to the Lord!' Then the Lord spoke to the fish, and it spewed Jonah out upon the dry land. (Jonah 1:15–2:10)

## Song

God moves in a mysterious way
his wonders to perform;
he plants his footsteps in the sea,
and rides upon the storm.

Deep in unfathomable mines
of never-failing skill
he treasures up his bright designs,
and works his sovereign will.

Ye fearful saints, fresh courage take;
the clouds ye so much dread
are big with mercy, and shall break
in blessings on your head.

Judge not the Lord by feeble sense,
but trust him for his grace;
behind a frowning providence
he hides a smiling face.

His purposes will ripen fast,
unfolding every hour;

the bud may have a bitter taste,
but sweet will be the flower.

Blind unbelief is sure to err,
and scan his work in vain;
God is his own interpreter,
and he will make it plain.

William Cowper, 1731–1800

## Prayer
Lord God of the watery depths, search us out, call us to do your will,
Amen.

❧

# EVENING PRAYER

## Greeting
A thousand ages in Thy sight
Are like an evening gone;
Short as the watch that ends the night
Before the rising sun.

Isaac Watts, 1674–1748

Some went down to the sea in ships, doing business on the
mighty waters; they saw the deeds of the Lord, his wondrous
works in the deep. (Psalm 107:23–4)

## Reflection
At eveningtime, Jesus walks alongside the sea. Everyone who is in
need is drawn to him. They gather in his presence and seek healing
from him. All are cured. We too can bring our sick and our lame to
him. We too can pray for healing. Tonight we bring all the weary
and weak of the world into the presence of Jesus. We walk along
the lakeside in their company and ask for his care.

## Reading
After Jesus had left that place, he passed along the Sea of
Galilee, and he went up the mountain, where he sat down. Great
crowds came to him, bringing with them the lame, the maimed,
the blind, the mute, and many others. They put them at his feet,

and he cured them, so that the crowd was amazed when they
saw the mute speaking, the maimed whole, the lame walking,
and the blind seeing. And they praised the God of Israel.
(Matthew 15:29–31)

## Song

At even, ere the sun was set,
the sick, O Lord, around thee lay;
O in what divers pains they met!
O with what joy they went away.

Once more 'tis eventide, and we
oppressed with various ills draw near;
what if thy form we cannot see
we know and feel that thou art here.

O Saviour Christ, our woes dispel;
for some are sick, and some are sad,
and some have never loved thee well,
and some have lost the love they had;

And some have found the world is vain,
yet from the world they break not free;
and some have friends who give them pain,
yet have not sought a friend in thee;

And none, O Lord, have perfect rest,
for none are wholly free from sin;
and they who fain would serve thee best
are conscious most of wrong within.

O Saviour Christ, thou too art man;
thou hast been troubled, tempted, tried;
thy kind but searching glance can scan
the very wounds that shame would hide;

Thy touch has still its ancient power;
no word from thee can fruitless fall:
hear, in this solemn evening hour,
and in thy mercy heal us all.

Henry Twells, 1823–1900

## Prayer
Lord Jesus, Son of the Living God, pour your Holy Spirit of healing on us now. Heal our world, Amen.

# ADVENT SUNDAYS

## MORNING PRAYER

### Greeting
There shall be endless peace for the throne of David and his kingdom. (Genesis 9:7)

Christ is born to renew the likeness that had been lost of old. The earth offers a cave to God, the Inaccessible One.
*Byzantine Daily Worship*

### Reflection
God blesses us with the mystery of our redemption. During Advent we reflect on the fact that we are restored to life and to grace by the birth of Jesus. He comes to us as one of us, and the world waits to make him welcome. We too, year by year, prepare our hearts and souls for his coming. 'Come, Lord Jesus, come.'

### Reading
Blessed be the God and Father of our Lord Jesus Christ, who has blessed us in Christ with every spiritual blessing in the heavenly places, just as he chose us in Christ before the foundation of the world to be holy and blameless before him in love. He destined us for adoption as his children through Jesus Christ, according to the good pleasure of his will, to the praise of his glorious grace that he freely bestowed on us in the Beloved. In him we have redemption through his blood, the forgiveness of our trespasses, according to the riches of his grace that he lavished on us. With all wisdom and insight he has made known to us the mystery of his will, according to his good pleasure that he set forth in Christ, as a plan for the fullness of time, to gather up all things in him, things in heaven and things on earth. (Ephesians 1:3–10)

## Song

Come, thou long-expected Jesus,
Born to set thy people free;
From our fears and sins release us;
Let us find our rest in thee.

Israel's strength and consolation,
Hope of all the earth thou art;
Dear desire of every nation,
Joy of every longing heart.

Born thy people to deliver;
Born a child, and yet a king;
Born to reign in us for ever;
Now thy gracious kingdom bring.

By thine own eternal Spirit
Rule in all our hearts alone;
By thine all-sufficient merit
Raise us to thy glorious throne.

Charles Wesley, 1707–88

## Prayer

Heavenly Lord, prepare our hearts and souls for your advent among us. Open our minds to receive the grace of your coming birth for our salvation, Amen.

❧

# EVENING PRAYER

## Greeting

In him we have redemption through his blood, the forgiveness of our trespasses. (Ephesians 1:7)

The tree of knowledge itself was good, and its fruit was good. For it was not the tree, as some think, but the disobedience, which had death in it.

Theophilus, second century

## Reflection

During the season of Advent, we think about the fact that we stand in need of the redemptive love of God. We acknowledge that this has been prepared for us from the beginning, when Adam and Eve first lost the life of paradise and the intimacy of the relationship with God that they enjoyed there. We recognise our need for a Saviour.

## Reading

They heard the sound of the Lord God walking in the garden at the time of the evening breeze, and the man and his wife hid themselves from the presence of the Lord God among the trees of the garden. But the Lord God called to the man, and said to him, 'Where are you?' He said, 'I heard the sound of you in the garden, and I was afraid, because I was naked; and I hid myself.' He said, 'Who told you that you were naked? Have you eaten from the tree of which I commanded you not to eat?' The man said, 'The woman whom you gave to be with me, she gave me fruit from the tree, and I ate.' Then the Lord God said to the woman, 'What is this that you have done?' The woman said, 'The serpent tricked me, and I ate.' (Genesis 3:8–13)

## Song

Adam lay ybounden
Bounden in a bond
Four thousand winter
Thought he not too long.

And all was for an apple,
An apple that he took,
As clerkes finden
Written in their book.

Ne had the apple taken been,
The apple taken been,
Ne had never Our Lady
A-been heavene Queen.

Blessed be the time
That apple taken was.
Therefore we moun singen
Deo gratias!

Medieval carol

## Prayer

Heavenly Lord, restore us to your grace; send your Son among us so that our hearts may be thankful and we may sing your praises, in the power of your Holy Spirit, this night and evermore, Amen.

# ADVENT MONDAYS

## MORNING PRAYER

### Greeting

'Greetings, favoured one! The Lord is with you.' (Luke 1:28)

Enter my humble life with its poverty and its limitations as you entered the stable of Bethlehem, the workshop of Nazareth, the cottage of Emmaus. Bless and consecrate the material of that small and ordinary life. Feed and possess my soul.

Evelyn Underhill, 1875–1941

### Reflection

With Mary, the mother of Jesus, we wait in silence, amidst the tasks of our everyday lives, confident that his angel will speak the word of life to us. We wait for his coming birth with some of her anticipation, confident that she will say to us, 'Do whatever he tells you' and that she will lead us to him.

### Reading

In the sixth month the angel Gabriel was sent by God to a town in Galilee called Nazareth, to a virgin engaged to a man whose name was Joseph, of the house of David. The virgin's name was Mary. And he came to her and said, 'Greetings, favoured one! The Lord is with you.' But she was much perplexed by his words and pondered what sort of greeting this might be. The angel said to her, 'Do not be afraid, Mary, for you have found favour with God. And now, you will conceive in your womb and bear a son, and you will name him Jesus. He will be great, and will be called the Son of the Most High, and the Lord God will give to him the throne of his ancestor David. He will reign over the house of Jacob forever, and of his kingdom there will be no end.' Mary said to the angel, 'How can this be, since I am a virgin?' The angel said to her, 'The Holy Spirit will come upon you, and the power of the Most High will overshadow you; therefore the child to be born will be holy; he will be called Son of God. And now, your relative Elizabeth in her old age has also conceived a son; and this is the sixth month for her who was said to be barren. For nothing will be impossible with God.' Then Mary said, 'Here am I, the servant of the Lord; let it be with me according to your word.' Then the angel departed from her. (Luke 1:26–38)

## Song

Mary the Dawn, Christ the perfect Day.
Mary the Gate, but Christ the heavenly Way.
Mary the Root, but Christ the mystic Vine.
Mary the Grape, but Christ the sacred Wine.
Mary the Corn-Sheaf, Christ the Living Bread.
Mary the Rose-Tree, Christ the Rose blood-red.
Mary the Fount, but Christ the cleansing Flood.
Mary the Chalice, but Christ the saving Blood.
Mary the Beacon, Christ the haven's Rest.
Mary the Mirror, Christ the Vision blest.

Source unknown

## Prayer

Lord Jesus Christ, born for our salvation, may your angels speak words of healing into our lives today. Help us to notice you wherever we are and whatever we are doing. Give us the diligence and strength of Mary, your mother, and keep us faithful to your word, Amen.

# EVENING PRAYER

## Greeting

'In the evening you will know that it was the Lord who brought you out of Egypt, and in the morning you will see the glory of the Lord.' (Exodus 16:6–7, NIV)

Those who seek the Lord shall praise Him. For those who seek shall find Him, and those who find Him shall praise Him. Let me seek Thee, Lord, in calling on Thee, and call on Thee in believing in Thee; for Thou hast been preached unto us.

St Augustine, 354–430

## Reflection

The gift of God is offered to us in the birth of Jesus for our redemption. Like Mary, we say 'yes' to the will of God, who comes to us in our need. We express our confidence by casting our care upon the Lord and preparing for the advent of our Saviour. We acknowledge that God comes to us because we are needy and worship him for his holiness, not our own.

## Reading

For while we were still weak, at the right time Christ died for the ungodly. Indeed, rarely will anyone die for a righteous person – though perhaps for a good person someone might actually dare to die. But God proves his love for us in that while we still were sinners Christ died for us. Much more surely then, now that we have been justified by his blood, will we be saved through him from the wrath of God. For if while we were enemies, we were reconciled to God through the death of his Son, much more surely, having been reconciled, will we be saved by his life. But more than that, we even boast in God through our Lord Jesus Christ, through whom we have now received reconciliation. (Romans 5:6–11)

## Song

O worship the Lord in the beauty of holiness!
Bow down before him, his glory proclaim;
with gold of obedience, and incense of lowliness,
kneel and adore him, the Lord is his name!

Low at his feet lay thy burden of carefulness,
high on his heart he will bear it for thee,
comfort thy sorrows, and answer thy prayerfulness,
guiding thy steps as may best for thee be.

Fear not to enter his courts in the slenderness
of the poor wealth thou wouldst reckon as thine:
truth in its beauty, and love in its tenderness,
these are the offerings to lay on his shrine.

These though we bring them in trembling and fearfulness,
he will accept for the name that is dear;
mornings of joy give for evenings of tearfulness,
trust for our trembling and hope for our fear.

O worship the Lord in the beauty of holiness!
Bow down before him, his glory proclaim;
with gold of obedience, and incense of lowliness,
kneel and adore him, the Lord is his name!

J. S. B. Monsell, 1811–75

## Prayer

Lord God of all beauty and all holiness, share the gifts of the life of faith with us. Renew our hope and charity and lead us to more generous service in your name, Amen.

# ADVENT TUESDAYS

## MORNING PRAYER

### Greeting

For while gentle silence enveloped all things, and night in its swift course was now half gone, thy all-powerful word leapt from heaven, from the royal throne, into the midst of the land that was doomed. (Wisdom of Solomon 18:14–15)

Let all the world in every corner sing
My God and King.

George Herbert, 1593–1633

### Reflection

The whole world awaits the all-powerful Word which is spoken into the midst of us, the Word which will renew the face of the earth by bringing Jesus to life in our lives. We wait in silent trust for the Word spoken from before the dawn of time to become incarnate in our own lives and circumstances.

### Reading

In the beginning was the Word, and the Word was with God, and the Word was God. He was in the beginning with God. All things came into being through him, and without him not one thing came into being. What has come into being in him was life, and the life was the light of all people. The light shines in the darkness, and the darkness did not overcome it. There was a man sent from God, whose name was John. He came as a witness to testify to the light, so that all might believe through him. He himself was not the light, but he came to testify to the light. The true light, which enlightens everyone, was coming into the world. He was in the world, and the world came into being through him; yet the world did not know him. He came to what was his own, and his own people did not accept him. But to all who received him, who believed in his name, he gave power to become children of God, who were born, not of blood or of the will of the flesh or of the will of man, but of God. And the Word became flesh and lived among us, and we have seen his glory, the glory as of a father's only son, full of grace and truth. (John 1:1–14)

## Song

Thou whose almighty Word
Chaos and darkness heard,
And took their flight;
Hear us, we humbly pray,
And where the Gospel day
Sheds not its glorious ray
Let there be light!

Thou who didst come to bring
On thy redeeming wing
Healing and sight,
Health to the sick in mind,
Sight to the inly blind,
Ah! Now to all mankind
Let there be light!

Spirit of light and love,
Life-giving, holy Dove,
Speed forth thy flight!
Move on the water's face,
Bearing the lamp of grace,
And in earth's darkest place
Let there be light!

Blessed and holy Three
Glorious Trinity,
Wisdom, Love, Might;
Boundless as ocean tide
Rolling in fullest pride,
Through the world far and wide
Let there be light!

John Marriott, 1780–1825

## Prayer

Beloved Lord Jesus, light for our eyes and word for our world; speak your message of hope and trust newly into our lives, so that our spirits may be raised to recognise you today and everyday, Amen.

❧

# EVENING PRAYER

## Greeting

'For all things come from you, and of your own have we given you.' (1 Chronicles 29:14)

David speaketh thus: *Dirigatur oratio mea sicut incensum* etc. — Let my prayer be dressed as incense in Thy sight. For even as incense that is cast into the fire maketh a sweet smell by the smoke rising up to the air, right so a Psalm savorly and softly sung or said in a burning heart, giveth up a sweet smell to the face of our Lord Jesus, and to all the Court of Heaven.

Walter Hilton, d. 1396

## Reflection

When we hear the Word of God, when Jesus is spoken into our lives, we are invited to listen, to hear, and to act upon what we hear. We respond to God by offering our lives in service and hope. We call upon the divine name and our prayer goes up like incense, smoke which curls up to heaven offering a sweet smell to the face of God. Alleluya, come, Lord, come.

## Reading

Once while Jesus was standing beside the lake of Gennesaret, and the crowd was pressing in on him to hear the word of God, he saw two boats there at the shore of the lake; the fishermen had gone out of them and were washing their nets. He got into one of the boats, the one belonging to Simon, and asked him to put out a little way from the shore. Then he sat down and taught the crowds from the boat. When he had finished speaking, he said to Simon, 'Put out into the deep water and let down your nets for a catch.' (Luke 5:1–4)

## Song

Lo! He comes with clouds descending,
Once for favoured sinners slain;
Thousand thousand Saints attending
Swell the triumph of his train:
Alleluya!
God appears, on earth to reign.

Every eye shall now behold him
Robed in dreadful majesty;
Those who set at nought and sold him,
Pierced and nailed him to the tree,
Deeply wailing
Shall the true Messiah see.

Those dear tokens of his passion
Still his dazzling body bears,
Cause of endless exultation
To his ransomed worshippers:
With what rapture
Gaze we on those glorious scars!

Yea, amen! Let all adore thee,
High on thine eternal throne;
Saviour, take the power and glory:
Claim the kingdom for thine own:
O come quickly!
Alleluya! Come, Lord, come!

Charles Wesley, 1707–88

## Prayer

We press to hear the word of God; we seek to go out into deep
waters; and now we pray to the Lord of heaven and earth to speak to
us and to call us to himself, Amen.

# ADVENT WEDNESDAYS

## MORNING PRAYER

### Greeting

> For the means of grace, and for the hope of glory.
> 'A General Thanksgiving', *Book of Common Prayer*

> Hope of all comfort, splendour of all aid,
> thou dost not fail nor leave the heart afraid.
> Robert Bridges, 1844–1930

### Reflection

Ours is often a world without hope, yet the spirit of Advent calls us
to live our lives with a sense of anticipation. Glory does lie ahead of
us, for we are all to experience the joy of heaven. Glory lies with us
now as well, for the Advent promise is that Jesus came and lived
among us, that he remains with us still and that he will come again in
the fullness of time.

### Reading

> Therefore, my friends, since we have confidence to enter the
> sanctuary by the blood of Jesus, by the new and living way that
> he opened for us through the curtain (that is, through his flesh),
> and since we have a great priest over the house of God, let us
> approach with a true heart in full assurance of faith, with our
> hearts sprinkled clean from an evil conscience and our bodies
> washed with pure water. Let us hold fast to the confession of
> our hope without wavering, for he who has promised is faithful.
> And let us consider how to provoke one another to love and
> good deeds, not neglecting to meet together, as is the habit of
> some, but encouraging one another, and all the more as you see
> the Day approaching. (Hebrews 10:19–25)

# Song

O come, O come, Emmanuel,
And ransom captive Israel,
That mourns in lonely exile here
Until the Son of God appear:
*Rejoice, rejoice!*
*Emmanuel shall come to thee, O Israel.*

O come, O come, thou Lord of might,
Who to thy tribes, on Sinai's height,
In ancient times didst give the law
In cloud, and majesty, and awe:
*Rejoice, rejoice . . .*

O come, thou Rod of Jesse, free
Thine own from Satan's tyranny;
From depth of hell thy people save,
And give them vict'ry o'er the grave:
*Rejoice, rejoice . . .*

O come, thou Key of David, come
And open wide our heav'nly home;
Make safe the way that leads on high,
And close the path to misery:
*Rejoice, rejoice . . .*

O come, thou Day-spring, come and cheer
Our spirits by thine advent here;
Disperse the gloomy clouds of night,
And death's dark shadows put to flight:
*Rejoice, rejoice . . .*
    Latin, eighteenth century, tr. John Mason Neale, 1818–66

# Prayer

Lord God of all our hope and anticipation, give us strength to put
our trust in you. Come to us now; draw aside the veil that separates
us from you and renew us for your service, Amen.

❧

# EVENING PRAYER

## Greeting

For everything created by God is good, and nothing is to be rejected, provided it is received with thanksgiving; for it is sanctified by God's word and by prayer. (1 Timothy 4:4–5)

To give and not to count the cost;
To fight and not to heed the wounds;
To toil and not to seek for rest.

Ignatius of Loyola, 1491–1556

## Reflection

When we celebrate the advent of Jesus into our world, we remember the generosity of God. For Jesus strips himself; he leaves behind the glory of heaven and embraces our humanity in its fullness. He is our example for he teaches us not to be afraid of our humanity but to embrace it in our turn.

## Reading

Let the same mind be in you that was in Christ Jesus, who, though he was in the form of God, did not regard equality with God as something to be exploited, but emptied himself, taking the form of a slave, being born in human likeness. And being found in human form, he humbled himself and became obedient to the point of death – even death on a cross. Therefore God also highly exalted him and gave him the name that is above every name, so that at the name of Jesus every knee should bend, in heaven and on earth and under the earth, and every tongue should confess that Jesus Christ is Lord, to the glory of God the Father. Therefore, my beloved, just as you have always obeyed me, not only in my presence, but much more now in my absence, work out your own salvation with fear and trembling; for it is God who is at work in you, enabling you both to will and to work for his good pleasure. Do all things without murmuring and arguing, so that you may be blameless and innocent, children of God without blemish in the midst of a crooked and perverse generation, in which you shine like stars in the world. (Philippians 2:5–15)

## Song

> Love divine, all loves excelling,
> Joy of heaven, to earth come down,
> fix in us thy humble dwelling,
> all thy faithful mercies crown.
> Jesu, thou art all compassion,
> pure unbounded love thou art;
> visit us with thy salvation,
> enter every trembling heart.
>
> Come, almighty, to deliver,
> let us all thy grace receive;
> suddenly return, and never,
> never more thy temple leave.
> Thee we would be always blessing,
> serve thee as thy host above;
> pray, and praise thee, without ceasing,
> glory in thy perfect love.
>
> Finish then thy new creation:
> pure and spotless let us be;
> let us see thy great salvation,
> perfectly restored in thee;
> changed from glory into glory,
> till in heaven we take our place,
> till we cast our crowns before thee,
> lost in wonder, love, and praise.

Charles Wesley, 1707–88

## Prayer

God of power and might, you sent your Son, Jesus Christ our Lord, to be our Saviour and our Redeemer. We pray today for the grace to be loving and to embrace our own humanity with the joy and simplicity with which he embraced his, Amen.

# ADVENT THURSDAYS

## MORNING PRAYER

### Greeting

A voice cries out: 'In the wilderness prepare the way of the Lord, make straight in the desert a highway for our God . . . Then the glory of the Lord shall be revealed, and all people shall see it together, for the mouth of the Lord has spoken.' (Isaiah 40:3, 5)

From strength unto strength we go forward on Sion's highway, to appear before God in the city of infinite day.

*Litany of St James*, tr. C. W. Humphreys

### Reflection

Advent is a time of preparation. We are to make straight the way of the Lord in our own lives. This means that we open our hearts to receive the glory of the Lord. Like John the Baptist, we have a task, for we are to tell others about the work of God in our lives. Like Jesus, we enter into the waters of baptism where we receive the gift of new life. When we emerge from this experience, we too will hear the voice of the Father: 'This is my beloved son', 'This is my beloved daughter'.

### Reading

In those days John the Baptist appeared in the wilderness of Judea, proclaiming, 'Repent, for the kingdom of heaven has come near.' This is the one of whom the prophet Isaiah spoke when he said, 'The voice of one crying out in the wilderness: "Prepare the way of the Lord, make his paths straight." ' Now John wore clothing of camel's hair with a leather belt around his waist, and his food was locusts and wild honey. Then the people of Jerusalem and all Judea were going out to him, and all the region along the Jordan, and they were baptized by him in the river Jordan, confessing their sins . . . [John said,] 'I baptize you with water for repentance, but one who is more powerful than I is coming after me; I am not worthy to carry his sandals. He will baptize you with the Holy Spirit and fire. His winnowing fork is in his hand, and he will clear his threshing floor and will gather his wheat into the granary; but the chaff he will burn with unquenchable fire.' Then Jesus came from Galilee to John at the Jordan, to be baptized by him. John would have prevented him, saying, 'I need to be baptized by you, and do you come to me?' But Jesus answered him, 'Let it be so now; for it is proper for us in this way to fulfil all righteousness.' Then he consented.

And when Jesus had been baptized, just as he came up from the water, suddenly the heavens were opened to him and he saw the Spirit of God descending like a dove and alighting on him. And a voice from heaven said, 'This is my Son, the Beloved, with whom I am well pleased.' (Matthew 3:1–6, 11–17)

## Song

On Jordan's bank the Baptist's cry
announces that the Lord is nigh;
awake, and hearken, for he brings
glad tidings of the King of kings.

Then cleansed be every breast from sin;
make straight the way for God within;
prepare we in our hearts a home,
where such a mighty guest may come.

For thou art our salvation, Lord,
our refuge, and our great reward;
without thy grace we waste away,
like flowers that wither and decay.

To heal the sick stretch out thine hand,
and bid the fallen sinner stand;
shine forth, and let thy light restore
Earth's own true loveliness once more.

All praise, eternal Son, to thee
whose advent doth thy people free,
whom with the Father we adore
and Holy Ghost for evermore.

Charles Coffin, 1676–1749, tr. J. Chandler, 1806–76

## Prayer

Heavenly Father, whose Spirit descended on Jesus at his baptism, come to us now. Renew our faith; confirm us in the certainty that we are your beloved sons and daughters, Amen.

# EVENING PRAYER

## Greeting

We will see him as he is. (1 John 3:2)

Embrace Christ born in our flesh, that you may deserve to see him also as the God of glory reigning in his majesty.

Leo the Great, d. 461

## Reflection

The birth of Jesus is a revelation to us, for when we 'see him as he is', we also see ourselves and our world more clearly. His coming transforms everything. The judgements we ordinarily make are turned upside down. This evening give yourself time to consider your own circumstances. Who are your friends, who are your enemies? Why? What values guide your decisions? Pray for the gifts of wisdom and understanding.

## Reading

A shoot shall come out from the stump of Jesse, and a branch shall grow out of his roots. The spirit of the Lord shall rest on him, the spirit of wisdom and understanding, the spirit of counsel and might, the spirit of knowledge and the fear of the Lord. His delight shall be in the fear of the Lord. He shall not judge by what his eyes see, or decide by what his ears hear; but with righteousness he shall judge the poor, and decide with equity for the meek of the earth; he shall strike the earth with the rod of his mouth, and with the breath of his lips he shall kill the wicked. Righteousness shall be the belt around his waist, and faithfulness the belt around his loins. The wolf shall live with the lamb, the leopard shall lie down with the kid, the calf and the lion and the fatling together, and a little child shall lead them. The cow and the bear shall graze, their young shall lie down together; and the lion shall eat straw like the ox. The nursing child shall play over the hole of the asp, and the weaned child shall put its hand on the adder's den. They will not hurt or destroy on all my holy mountain; for the earth will be full of the knowledge of the Lord as the waters cover the sea. (Isaiah 11:1–9)

## Song

Hark, a thrilling voice is sounding;
'Christ is nigh', it seems to say;
'Cast away the dreams of darkness,
O ye children of the day.'

Wakened by the solemn warning,
Let the earth-bound soul arise;
Christ, her sun, all ill dispelling,
Shines upon the morning skies.

Lo, the Lamb, so long-expected
Comes with pardon down from heaven;
Let us haste with tears of sorrow,
One and all to be forgiven;

That when next he comes with glory,
And the world is wrapped in fear,
With his mercy he may shield us,
And with words of love draw near.

Honour, might, and blessing
To the Father and the Son,
With the everlasting Spirit,
While eternal ages run.

Latin, sixth century, tr. Edward Caswall, 1814–78

## Prayer

Lord of heaven and earth, give us sight of your glory; enable us to
see you as you are in our lives; open our hearts to understand your
ways. Give us your wisdom and understanding, Amen.

# ADVENT FRIDAYS

## MORNING PRAYER

### Greeting

They looked towards the desert, and there was the glory of the Lord appearing in the cloud. (Exodus 16:10, NIV)

O may this bounteous God
through all our life be near us.

Martin Rinkart, 1586–1649

### Reflection

Jesus is born within time, as part of the rhythm of the hours of our universe. We greet him with all the fervour of the shepherds and go to the waiting manger to offer our gifts. The simplicity of the gospel narrative is deceptive for it is determined to show to us that God uses the ordinary things of human life – like a census, or a crowded inn – to break through to us. Let us, like the shepherds, listen for the sound of angel voices as the dynamics of heaven meet those of earth.

### Reading

In those days a decree went out from Emperor Augustus that all the world should be registered. This was the first registration and was taken while Quirinius was governor of Syria. All went to their own towns to be registered. Joseph also went from the town of Nazareth in Galilee to Judea, to the city of David called Bethlehem, because he was descended from the house and family of David. He went to be registered with Mary, to whom he was engaged and who was expecting a child. While they were there, the time came for her to deliver her child. And she gave birth to her firstborn son and wrapped him in bands of cloth, and laid him in a manger, because there was no place for them in the inn. In that region there were shepherds living in the fields, keeping watch over their flock by night. Then an angel of the Lord stood before them, and the glory of the Lord shone around them, and they were terrified. But the angel said to them, 'Do not be afraid; for see – I am bringing you good news of great joy for all the people: to you is born this day in the city of David a Saviour, who is the Messiah, the Lord. This will be a sign for you: you will find a child wrapped in bands of cloth and lying in a manger.' And suddenly there was with the angel a multitude of the heavenly host, praising God and saying, 'Glory to God in the highest heaven, and on earth peace among those whom he favours!' (Luke 2:1–14)

## Song

Hills of the north, rejoice,
river and mountain-spring,
hark to the advent voice;
valley and lowland, sing.
Christ comes in righteousness and love,
he brings salvation from above.

Isles of the southern seas,
sing to the listening earth;
carry on every breeze
hope of a world's new birth:
in Christ shall all be made anew;
his word is sure, his promise true.

Lands of the East, arise,
he is your brightest morn,
greet him with joyous eyes,
praise shall his path adorn:
the God whom you have longed to know
in Christ draws near, and calls you now.

Shores of the utmost west,
lands of the setting sun,
welcome the heavenly guest
in whom the dawn has come:
he brings a never-ending light,
who triumphed o'er our darkest night.

Shout, as you journey home;
songs be in every mouth!
Lo, from the north they come,
from east and west and south:
in Jesus all shall find their rest,
in him the universe be blest.

Charles E. Oakley, 1832–65

## Prayer

'In Jesus all shall find their rest.' Help us, Lord, to seek and find our rest in you. Call us to the manger as insistently as once your angels called the shepherds, that we too may praise your glory and sing with their voices, Amen.

❧

# EVENING PRAYER

## Greeting

Sing and rejoice, O daughter Zion! For lo, I will come and dwell in your midst, says the Lord. (Zechariah 2:10)

God himself, who is almighty, the Creator of all things, and invisible, has sent from heaven, and placed among us, him who is the truth, and the holy and incomprehensible Word, and has firmly established him in our hearts.

Anon., second century

## Reflection

Jesus, who is placed in our hearts as surely as he is placed in the manger in Bethlehem, is the child of the promise. He is God's elect, and he comes and dwells in the midst of us. During Advent, we have time to reflect on the indwelling presence of the Lord in our own lives. We are his cradle, his Bethlehem for he is born in us too.

## Reading

But you, O Bethlehem of Ephrathah, who are one of the little clans of Judah, from you shall come forth for me one who is to rule in Israel, whose origin is from of old, from ancient days. Therefore he shall give them up until the time when she who is in labour has brought forth; then the rest of his kindred shall return to the people of Israel. And he shall stand and feed his flock in the strength of the Lord, in the majesty of the name of the Lord his God. And they shall live secure, for now he shall be great to the ends of the earth; and he shall be the one of peace. (Micah 5:2–5)

## Song

See amid the winter's snow,
born for us on earth below;
see the tender Lamb appears,
promised from eternal years:
*Hail, thou ever-blessed morn!*
*Hail, redemption's happy dawn!*
*Sing through all Jerusalem,*
*Christ is born in Bethlehem.*

Lo, within a manger lies
he who built the starry skies;
he who, throned in height sublime,
sits amid the cherubim:
*Hail, thou ever-blessed morn . . .*

Say, ye holy shepherds, say
what your joyful news today;
wherefore have ye left your sheep
on the lonely mountain steep?
*Hail, thou ever-blessed morn . . .*

'As we watched at dead of night,
lo, we saw a wondrous light;
angels singing "Peace on earth"
told us of the Saviour's birth.'
*Hail, thou ever-blessed morn . . .*

Sacred infant, all divine,
what a tender love was thine,
thus to come from highest bliss
down to such a world as this!
*Hail, thou ever-blessed morn . . .*

Teach, O teach us, Holy Child,
by thy face so meek and mild,
teach us to resemble thee,
in thy sweet humility.
*Hail, thou ever-blessed morn* . . .

Edward Caswall, 1814–78

## Prayer

Come, Lord Jesus, come. Fill our hearts with love for you and for
our neighbour. Help us to resolve never to cast you out but always
to remain open to your will. Dwell in us now and evermore, Amen.

# ADVENT SATURDAYS

## MORNING PRAYER

### Greeting

'I wait for your salvation, O Lord.' (Genesis 49:18)

You cannot glory in the Cross of our Lord Jesus Christ while you trust in treasures laid up on earth: you cannot taste and see how gracious the Lord is, while you are hungering for gold. If you have not rejoiced at the thought of his coming, that day will be indeed a day of wrath to you.

Bernard of Clairvaux, 1090–1153

### Reflection

The day of the Lord's coming is a day of joy and a day of judgement. For light is cast on our world and the gaps between God's will for us and our own actions stand out in perspective. Yet the Lord who comes and who stands in judgement over us is also our redeemer. That is why today is a day of joy: for the coming of the day of the Lord is about forgiveness, freedom and love.

### Reading

The people who walked in darkness have seen a great light; those who lived in a land of deep darkness – on them light has shined. You have multiplied the nation, you have increased its joy; they rejoice before you as with joy at the harvest, as people exult when dividing plunder. For the yoke of their burden, and the bar across their shoulders, the rod of their oppressor, you have broken as on the day of Midian. For all the boots of the tramping warriors and all the garments rolled in blood shall be burned as fuel for the fire. For a child has been born for us, a son given to us; authority rests upon his shoulders; and he is named Wonderful Counsellor, Mighty God, Everlasting Father,

Prince of Peace. His authority shall grow continually, and there shall be endless peace for the throne of David and his kingdom. He will establish and uphold it with justice and with righteousness from this time onward and forevermore. The zeal of the Lord of hosts will do this. (Isaiah 9:2–7)

## Song

Brightest and best of the sons of the morning,
dawn on our darkness, and lend us thine aid;
star of the east, the horizon adorning,
guide where our infant redeemer is laid.

Cold on his cradle the dew-drops are shining;
low lies his head with the beasts of the stall;
angels adore him in slumber reclining,
maker and monarch and saviour of all.

Say, shall we yield him, in costly devotion,
odours of Edom, and offerings divine,
gems of the mountain, and pearls of the ocean,
myrrh from the forest, or gold from the mine?

Vainly we offer each ample oblation,
vainly with gifts would his favour secure:
richer by far is the heart's adoration,
dearer to God are the prayers of the poor.

Brightest and best of the sons of the morning,
dawn on our darkness, and lend us thine aid;
star of the east, the horizon adorning,
guide where our infant redeemer is laid.

Reginald Heber, 1783–1826

## Prayer

Lord Jesus Christ, you come among us to bring judgement on our world; forgive us for all that lies behind us and call us to a new future in your service and love, Amen.

ॐ

# EVENING PRAYER

## Greeting

And the Word became flesh and lived among us, and we have
seen his glory, the glory as of the Father's only Son, full of grace
and truth. (John 1:14)

'See! I am God: see! I am in all thing: see! I do all thing: see! I
lift never mine hands off my works, nor ever shall, without end:
see! I lead all thing to the end I ordained it to be from without
beginning, by the same Might, Wisdom and Love whereby I
made it. How should any thing be amiss?'

Julian of Norwich, c. 1342–1413

## Reflection

'Amen. O come, Lord Jesus.' The final words of the Bible remind us
of the importance of praying for the return of our Saviour. He is the
Alpha and the Omega, the beginning and end of all things, the Lord
who brought us into being, the Lord to whom we will return. All
shall be well, for nothing is now amiss.

## Reading

'See, I am coming soon; my reward is with me, to repay according to everyone's work. I am the Alpha and the Omega, the first
and the last, the beginning and the end' . . . 'It is I, Jesus, who
sent my angel to you with this testimony for the churches. I am
the root and the descendant of David, the bright morning star.'
The Spirit and the bride say, 'Come.' And let everyone who
hears say, 'Come.' And let everyone who is thirsty come. Let
anyone who wishes take the water of life as a gift. I warn
everyone who hears the words of the prophecy of this book: if
anyone adds to them, God will add to that person the plagues
described in this book; if anyone takes away from the words of
the book of this prophecy, God will take away that person's
share in the tree of life and in the holy city, which are described
in this book. The one who testifies to these things says, 'Surely
I am coming soon.' Amen. Come, Lord Jesus! The grace of the
Lord Jesus be with all the saints. Amen. (Revelation 22:12–13,
16–21)

# Song

Drop down, ye heavens, from above, and let the skies pour down righteousness.

Be not wroth very sore, O Lord, neither remember iniquity for ever: thy holy cities are a wilderness, Sion is a wilderness, Jerusalem a desolation: our holy and our beautiful house, where our fathers praised thee. We have sinned, and are as an unclean thing, and we all do fade as a leaf: and our iniquities, like the wind, have taken us away; thou hast hid thy face from us: and hast consumed us, because of our iniquities.

Ye are my witnesses, saith the Lord, and my servant whom I have chosen: that ye may know me and believe me: I, even I, am the Lord, and beside me there is no saviour: and there is none that can deliver out of my hand.

Comfort ye, comfort ye my people; my salvation shall not tarry: I have blotted out as a thick cloud thy transgressions: fear not, for I will save thee: for I am the Lord thy God, the holy one of Israel, thy redeemer.

*Rorate Caeli*

# Prayer

We pray for the salvation of our world, for the restoration of good things, for a sense that all shall indeed be well. Heavenly Lord, born among us, grant us this, Amen.

# LENT SUNDAYS

## MORNING PRAYER

### Greeting

Four seasons fill the measure of the year;
There are four seasons in the mind of man.

John Keats, 1795–1821

For everything there is a season, and a time for every matter
under heaven: a time to be born, and a time to die; a time to
plant, and a time to pluck up what is planted; a time to kill, and
a time to heal; a time to break down, and a time to build up.
(Ecclesiastes 3:1–3)

### Reflection

Lent is a solemn season, a time when we contemplate the great
mysteries of our faith and receive a deeper understanding of the
great work that Jesus did in saving us from the consequences of our
sins. Our own celebration of Lent brings us into the presence of
God. We stand with the prophet Isaiah and hear the words, 'Your
guilt has departed; your sin is blotted out.'

### Reading

In the year that King Uzziah died, I saw the Lord sitting on a
throne, high and lofty; and the hem of his robe filled the temple.
Seraphs were in attendance above him; each had six wings:
with two they covered their faces, and with two they covered
their feet, and with two they flew. And one called to another
and said: 'Holy, holy, holy is the Lord of hosts; the whole earth
is full of his glory.' The pivots on the thresholds shook at the
voices of those who called, and the house filled with smoke.
And I said: 'Woe is me! I am lost, for I am a man of unclean lips,
and I live among a people of unclean lips; yet my eyes have seen

the King, the Lord of hosts!' Then one of the seraphs flew to me, holding a live coal that had been taken from the altar with a pair of tongs. The seraph touched my mouth with it and said: 'Now that this has touched your lips, your guilt has departed and your sin is blotted out.' Then I heard the voice of the Lord saying, 'Whom shall I send, and who will go for us?' And I said, 'Here am I; send me!' (Isaiah 6:1–8)

## Song

Let all mortal flesh keep silence, and with fear and trembling
    stand;
Ponder nothing earthly-minded, for with blessing in his hand
Christ our God to earth descended, our full homage to
    demand.

King of kings, yet born of Mary, as of old on earth he stood,
Lord of lords, in human vesture – in the body and the
    blood –
He will give to all his faithful his own self for heavenly food.

Rank on rank the host of heaven spreads its vanguard on the
    way,
As the Light of light descendeth from the realms of endless
    day,
That the powers of hell may vanish as the darkness clears
    away.

At his feet the six-winged seraph; cherubim with sleepless eye
Veil their faces to the Presence, as with ceaseless voice they
    cry –
Alleluia, alleluia, alleluia, Lord most high!
        From the *Liturgy of St James*, tr. G. Moultrie, 1829–85

## Prayer

Heavenly God, whose Son came among us for our redemption, prepare our hearts and minds to keep the holy season of Lent. Call us to repentance, and to hope, by the power of your Holy Spirit, Amen.

❧

# EVENING PRAYER

## Greeting

Lighten our darkness, we beseech thee, O Lord.

*The Book of Common Prayer*

O thou that hearest prayer, unto thee shall all flesh come. (Psalm 65:2, KJV)

## Reflection

During Lent we reflect on the true nature of freedom. It is not licentiousness, or doing just what you want or what you feel like. The Christian life is a disciplined life, one which is modelled on the life of Jesus. We live in the confidence that we are saved and seek to follow the Spirit of Christ.

## Reading

There is therefore now no condemnation for those who are in Christ Jesus. For the law of the Spirit of life in Christ Jesus has set you free from the law of sin and of death. For God has done what the law, weakened by the flesh, could not do: by sending his own Son in the likeness of sinful flesh, and to deal with sin, he condemned sin in the flesh, so that the just requirement of the law might be fulfilled in us, who walk not according to the flesh but according to the Spirit. For those who live according to the flesh set their minds on the things of the flesh, but those who live according to the Spirit set their minds on the things of the Spirit. To set the mind on the flesh is death, but to set the mind on the Spirit is life and peace. For this reason the mind that is set on the flesh is hostile to God; it does not submit to God's law – indeed it cannot, and those who are in the flesh cannot please God. But you are not in the flesh; you are in the Spirit, since the Spirit of God dwells in you. Anyone who does not have the Spirit of Christ does not belong to him. But if Christ is in you, though the body is dead because of sin, the Spirit is life because of righteousness. If the Spirit of him who raised Jesus from the dead dwells in you, he who raised Christ from the dead will give life to your mortal bodies also through his Spirit that dwells in you. (Romans 8:1–11)

## Song

Come, my Way, my Truth, my Life:
Such a Way, as gives us breath;
Such a Truth, as ends all strife;
Such a Life, as killeth death.

Come, my Light, my Feast, my Strength:
Such a Light, as shows a feast;
Such a Feast, as mends in length;
Such a Strength, as makes his guest.

Come my Joy, my Love, my Heart:
Such a Joy, as none can move;
Such a Love, as none can part;
Such a Heart, as joys in love.

George Herbert, 1593–1633

## Prayer

We pray in the confidence that there is no condemnation for those
who are in Christ Jesus: strengthen our resolve to live according to
the life of the Spirit, Amen.

# LENT MONDAYS

## MORNING PRAYER

### Greeting

Rejoice always, pray without ceasing, give thanks in all circumstances; for this is the will of God in Christ Jesus for you. (1 Thessalonians 5:16–18)

When I survey the wondrous Cross,
On which the Prince of Glory died,
My richest gain I count but loss
And pour contempt on all my pride.

Isaac Watts, 1674–1748

### Reflection

The Lenten call is to prayer, fasting and almsgiving. Today we reflect on the prayer of Jesus who holds us up to the Father and assures us that we are made for glory and for love. At the final meal which he shared with his friends Jesus prays for his disciples and he prays for us.

### Reading

[Jesus] looked towards heaven and prayed: ' . . . My prayer is not for them alone. I pray also for those who will believe in me through their message, that all of them may be one, Father, just as you are in me and I am in you. May they also be in us so that the world may believe that you have sent me. I have given them the glory that you gave me, that they may be one as we are one: I in them and you in me. May they be brought to complete unity to let the world know that you sent me and have loved them even as you have loved me. Father, I want those you have given me to be with me where I am, and to see my glory, the glory you have given me because you loved me before the creation of the world. Righteous Father, though the world does not know you, I know you, and they know that you have sent me. I have made you known to them, and will continue to make you known in order that the love you have for me may be in them and that I myself may be in them.' (John 17:1, 20–6, NIV)

## Song

Love bade me welcome: yet my soul drew back,
    Guilty of dust and sin.
But sweet-ey'd Love, observing me grow slack
    From my first entrance in,
Drew nearer to me, sweetly questioning,
    If I lack'd any thing.

A guest, I answer'd, worthy to be here:
    Love said, You shall be he.
I the unkind, ungrateful? Ah my dear,
    I cannot look on thee.
Love took my hand, and smiling did reply,
    Who made the eyes but I?

Truth, Lord, but I have marr'd them: let my shame
    Go where it doth deserve.
And know you not, says Love, who bore the blame?
    My dear, then I will serve.
You must sit down, says Love, and taste my meat:
    So I did sit and eat.

George Herbert, 1593–1633

## Prayer

Heavenly Father, your Son Jesus Christ prays for us and calls us to pray at all times, stir us up so that we may believe in the power of your Holy Spirit who prays within us, Amen.

ఈౡ

# EVENING PRAYER

## Greeting
 O world invisible, we view thee,
 O world intangible, we touch thee,
 O world unknowable, we know thee.
Francis Thompson, 1859–1907

 Delight in the Almighty, and lift up your face to God. You will
 pray to him, and he will hear you, and you will pay your vows.
 (Job 22:26–7)

## Reflection
Prayer is not simply about effort; it is a source of joy as Paul reminds
his followers in Philippi. We have an opportunity to centre our prayer
on the saving work of Jesus when we reflect on our redemption. We
are offered the chance of renewal as we think about everything which
is true, honourable, just and pure.

## Reading
 Rejoice in the Lord always; again I will say, Rejoice. Let your
 gentleness be known to everyone. The Lord is near. Do not
 worry about anything, but in everything by prayer and supplica-
 tion with thanksgiving let your requests be made known to God.
 And the peace of God, which surpasses all understanding, will
 guard your hearts and your minds in Christ Jesus. Finally,
 beloved, whatever is true, whatever is honourable, whatever is
 just, whatever is pure, whatever is pleasing, whatever is com-
 mendable, if there is any excellence and if there is anything
 worthy of praise, think about these things. Keep on doing the
 things that you have learned and received and heard and seen
 in me, and the God of peace will be with you. (Philippians 4:4–
 9)

## Song
 Be thou my vision, O Lord of my heart,
 Be all else but naught to me, save that thou art;
 Be thou my best thought in the day and the night,
 Both waking and sleeping, thy presence my light.

High King of heaven, thou heaven's bright Sun,
O grant me its joys after vict'ry is won;
Great heart of my own heart, whatever befall,
Still be my vision, O Ruler of all.

Irish, eighth century, tr. Mary Byrne, 1880–1931

## Prayer
We pray to the Ruler of All, that our vision may be renewed and we may experience the joy of discipleship; Lord God, be our best thought and call us to yourself, Amen.

# LENT TUESDAYS

## MORNING PRAYER

### Greeting

In the beginning when God created the heavens and the earth, the earth was a formless void and darkness covered the face of the deep, while a wind from God swept over the face of the waters. (Genesis 1:1–2)

All sins are attempts to fill voids.

Simone Weil, 1909–43

### Reflection

We need not be afraid of hunger or emptiness, for God will create where there is nothingness. The ancient Lenten discipline of fasting reminds us that how we live is part of our Christian discipleship. If we are inspired by the insights of the gospel, then everything is brought into the frame. God nourishes and nurtures us, so during Lent we remember to give thanks for our food and we resolve to share what we have with other people. We submit our lifestyle to scrutiny in the confidence that God who knows and loves us also calls us to repentance.

### Reading

'And whenever you fast, do not look dismal, like the hypocrites, for they disfigure their faces so as to show others that they are fasting. Truly I tell you, they have received their reward. But when you fast, put oil on your head and wash your face, so that your fasting may be seen not by others but by your Father who is in secret; and your Father who sees in secret will reward you. Do not store up for yourselves treasures on earth, where moth and rust consume and where thieves break in and steal; but store up for yourselves treasures in heaven, where neither moth nor rust consumes and where thieves do not break in and steal. For where your treasure is, there your heart will be also. The eye is the lamp of the body. So, if your eye is healthy, your whole body will be full of light; but if your eye is unhealthy, your whole body will be full of darkness. If then the light in you is darkness, how great is the darkness! No one can serve two masters; for a slave will either hate the one and love the other, or be devoted to the one and despise the other. You cannot serve God and wealth.' (Matthew 6:16–24)

## Song

King of glory, King of peace,
    I will love thee;
And that love may never cease,
    I will move thee.
Thou hast granted my request,
    Thou hast heard me;
Thou didst note my working breast;
    Thou hast spared me.

Wherefore with my utmost art
    I will sing thee,
And the cream of all my heart
    I will bring thee.
Though my sins against me cried,
    Thou didst clear me;
And alone, when they replied,
    Thou didst hear me.

Seven whole days, not one in seven,
    I will praise thee;
In my heart, though not in heaven,
    I can raise thee.
Small it is, in this poor sort
    To enrol thee:
E'en eternity's too short
    To extol thee.

George Herbert, 1593–1632

## Prayer

Heavenly Father, Giver of all that we have and are and do, come to us now. Call us to your service and to your praise, Amen.

࿔

# EVENING PRAYER

## Greeting

Remove far from me falsehood and lying; give me neither poverty nor riches; feed me with the food that I need, or I shall be full, and deny you, and say, 'Who is the Lord?' or I shall be poor, and steal, and profane the name of my God. (Proverbs 30:8–9)

Search well another world; who studies this,
Travels in clouds, seeks manna, where none is.

Henry Vaughan, 1622–95

## Reflection

Whether we are rich or poor, Jesus calls us to simplicity and to freedom. We are not to fret or to be troubled for we are more than what we own or what we eat. As spiritual beings, we have a destiny which transcends our present life and reminds us of our unique dignity as the beloved sons and daughters of God. During Lent, we reflect on the true meaning of fasting, for it is about being open to receive the gifts of God.

## Reading

'Therefore I tell you, do not worry about your life, what you will eat or what you will drink, or about your body, what you will wear. Is not life more than food, and the body more than clothing? Look at the birds of the air; they neither sow nor reap nor gather into barns, and yet your heavenly Father feeds them. Are you not of more value than they? And can any of you by worrying add a single hour to your span of life? And why do you worry about clothing? Consider the lilies of the field, how they grow; they neither toil nor spin, yet I tell you, even Solomon in all his glory was not clothed like one of these. But if God so clothes the grass of the field, which is alive today and tomorrow is thrown into the oven, will he not much more clothe you – you of little faith? Therefore do not worry, saying, "What will we eat?" or "What will we drink?" or "What will we wear?" For it is the Gentiles who strive for all these things; and indeed your heavenly Father knows that you need all these things. But strive first for the kingdom of God and his righteousness, and all these things will be given to you as well. So do not worry about tomorrow, for tomorrow will bring worries of its own. Today's trouble is enough for today.' (Matthew 6:25–34)

## Song

O Father, give the spirit power to climb
To the fountain of all light, and be purified.
Break through the mists of earth, the weight of the clod,
Shine forth in splendour, thou that art calm weather,
And quiet resting place for faithful souls.
To see thee is the end and the beginning,
Thou carriest us, and thou dost go before.
Thou art the journey, and the journey's end.

Boethius, 480–524, tr. Helen Waddell, 1889–1965

## Prayer

Lord of the journey, of all that holds us in being and all that sustains us, come to us now. Set us free from fear and call us to yourself, Amen.

# LENT WEDNESDAYS

## MORNING PRAYER

### Greeting
Give us the wings of faith
to rise within the veil.

Isaac Watts, 1674–1748

'Give us this day our daily bread.' (Matthew 6:11)

### Reflection
When we are driven by a higher dream, we remember that the generosity of God in giving us our daily bread has to be mirrored in our generosity when we bring our gifts and riches and return them to God, from whom they come. Generosity makes us human. May all our offerings be freewill-offerings, given to all for the glory of God.

### Reading
The leaders of ancestral houses made their freewill-offerings, as did also the leaders of the tribes, the commanders of the thousands and of the hundreds, and the officers over the king's work. They gave for the service of the house of God five thousand talents and ten thousand darics of gold, ten thousand talents of silver, eighteen thousand talents of bronze, and one hundred thousand talents of iron. Whoever had precious stones gave them to the treasury of the house of the Lord, into the care of Jehiel the Gershonite. Then the people rejoiced because these had given willingly, for with single mind they had offered freely to the Lord; King David also rejoiced greatly. Then David blessed the Lord in the presence of all the assembly; David said: 'Blessed are you, O Lord, the God of our ancestor Israel, for ever and ever. Yours, O Lord, are the greatness, the power,

the glory, the victory, and the majesty; for all that is in the heavens and on the earth is yours; yours is the kingdom, O Lord, and you are exalted as head above all. Riches and honour come from you, and you rule over all. In your hand are power and might; and it is in your hand to make great and to give strength to all. And now, our God, we give thanks to you and praise your glorious name. But who am I, and what is my people, that we should be able to make this freewill-offering? For all things come from you, and of your own have we given you.'
(1 Chronicles 29:6–14)

## Song

O thou who camest from above
The pure celestial fire to impart,
Kindle a flame of sacred love
On the mean altar of my heart!

There let it for thy glory burn
With inextinguishable blaze,
And trembling to its source return,
In humble love and fervent praise.

Jesus, confirm my heart's desire
To work, and speak, and think for thee;
Still let me guard the holy fire,
And still stir up thy gift in me.

Still let me prove thy perfect will,
My acts of faith and love repeat,
Till death thy endless mercies seal,
And make the sacrifice complete.

Charles Wesley, 1707–88

## Prayer

We offer our hearts to become an altar of sacrifice to God. Beloved Lord, inspire in us the generosity that will lead us to serve your world, Amen.

❧

# EVENING PRAYER

## Greeting

'Blessed are the poor in spirit: for theirs is the kingdom of heaven.' (Matthew 5:3)

Cover my defenceless head
With the shadow of thy wing.

Charles Wesley, 1707–88

## Reflection

We thank God for the glory of our destiny, secured by the redemptive work of Christ. We receive the gift of his love and grace and resolve to share the glorious inheritance which is now ours. Christ is our hope and we praise him with thankful hearts. Christ is the hope of our world, so we resolve to give to others as generously as we have received.

## Reading

In Christ we have also obtained an inheritance, having been destined according to the purpose of him who accomplishes all things according to his counsel and will, so that we, who were the first to set our hope on Christ, might live for the praise of his glory. In him you also, when you had heard the word of truth, the gospel of your salvation, and had believed in him, were marked with the seal of the promised Holy Spirit; this is the pledge of our inheritance towards redemption as God's own people, to the praise of his glory. I have heard of your faith in the Lord Jesus and your love towards all the saints, and for this reason I do not cease to give thanks for you as I remember you in my prayers. (Ephesians1:11–16)

## Song

Let folly praise what fancy loves,
I praise and love that Child,
Whose heart no thought, whose tongue no word,
Whose hand no deed defiled.
I praise him most, I love him best,
All praise and love is his;

While him I love, in him I live,
And cannot live amiss.

Love's sweetest mark, laud's highest theme,
Man's most desiréd light,
To love him, life, to leave him, death,
To live in him, delight.
He mine by gift, I his by debt,
Thus each to other due,
First friend he was, best friend he is,
All times will find him true.

Though young, yet wise, though small, yet strong,
Though Man, yet God he is;
As wise he knows, as strong he can,
As God he loves to bless.
His knowledge rules, his strength defends,
His love doth cherish all;
His birth our joy, his life our light,
His death our end of thrall.

Robert Southwell SJ, 1561–95

## Prayer

We pray to Christ, our friend and brother: Beloved Lord Jesus, free
us from every thrall, especially from the fear which might make us
less than generous with you and with our world, Amen.

# LENT THURSDAYS

## MORNING PRAYER

### Greeting

Since wars begin in the minds of men, it is in the minds of men that the defences of peace must be constructed.

UNESCO Constitution, adopted 16 November 1945

A new heart I will give you, and a new spirit I will put within you; and I will remove from your body the heart of stone and give you a heart of flesh. (Ezekiel 36:26)

### Reflection

Lent gives us the opportunity to take stock of our lives, to evaluate our priorities, to accept ourselves as we are and to resolve to do better. This kind of conversion means being honest with ourselves and with God. The psalmist repents of his sins and receives forgiveness. This is painful stuff but infinitely worthwhile. Today we can start again. We bring our contrite hearts to God.

### Reading

Have mercy on me, O God, according to your steadfast love; according to your abundant mercy blot out my transgressions. Wash me thoroughly from my iniquity, and cleanse me from my sin. For I know my transgressions, and my sin is ever before me. Against you, you alone, have I sinned, and done what is evil in your sight, so that you are justified in your sentence and blameless when you pass judgement. Indeed, I was born guilty, a sinner when my mother conceived me. You desire truth in the inward being; therefore teach me wisdom in my secret heart. Purge me with hyssop, and I shall be clean; wash me, and I shall be whiter than snow. Let me hear joy and gladness; let the bones that you have crushed rejoice. Hide your face from my sins, and blot out all my iniquities. Create in me a clean heart, O God, and put a new and right spirit within me. Do not cast me away from your presence, and do not take your holy spirit from me. Restore to me the joy of your salvation, and sustain in me a willing spirit. Then I will teach transgressors your ways, and sinners will return to you. Deliver me from bloodshed, O God, O God of my salvation, and my tongue will sing aloud of your deliverance. O Lord, open my lips, and my mouth will declare your praise. For you have no delight in sacrifice; if I were to give a burnt offering, you would not be pleased. The sacrifice acceptable to God is a broken spirit; a broken and contrite heart, O God, you will not despise. Do good to Zion in your good pleasure; rebuild the walls of Jerusalem, then you will delight in right sacrifices, in burnt offerings and whole burnt offerings; then bulls will be offered on your altar. (Psalm 51:1–19)

## Song

Jesu, the very thought of thee,
With sweetness fills my breast;
But sweeter far thy face to see,
And in thy presence rest.

Nor voice can sing, nor heart can frame,
Nor can the memory find,
A sweeter sound than thy blest Name,
O Saviour of mankind.

O hope of every contrite heart,
O joy of all the meek,
To those who fall, how kind thou art,
How good to those who seek!

But what to those who find? Ah! this
Nor tongue nor pen can show:
The love of Jesus, what it is
None but his loved ones know.

Jesu, our only joy be thou,
As thou our prize wilt be;
Jesu, be thou our glory now,

And through eternity.

Twelfth century, tr. Edward Caswall, 1814–78

## Prayer

Lord Jesus Christ, hope of every contrite heart, source of all grace, we turn to you now asking your forgiveness. Come to us with healing on your wings, Amen.

๑๕

# EVENING PRAYER

## Greeting

Love is God, and to die means that I, a particle of love, shall return to the general and eternal source.

Leo Tolstoy, 1828–1910

God is love, and those who abide in love abide in God, and God abides in them. Love has been perfected among us in this: that we may have boldness on the day of judgement, because as he is, so are we in this world. (1 John 4:16–17)

## Reflection

The call to repentance is a call to joy, to a life of love and of blessing. When we acknowledge our sins and turn to God for forgiveness, then we are offered a fresh beginning. We are to be alive to the goodness of God in new ways and to trust in the divine mercy which is revealed to us. God is good; God desires our goodness too. God is merciful; we too must show mercy.

## Reading

Finally, all of you, have unity of spirit, sympathy, love for one another, a tender heart, and a humble mind. Do not repay evil for evil or abuse for abuse; but, on the contrary, repay with a blessing. It is for this that you were called – that you might inherit a blessing. For 'Those who desire life and desire to see good days, let them keep their tongues from evil and their lips from speaking deceit; let them turn away from evil and do good; let them seek peace and pursue it. For the eyes of the Lord are on the righteous, and his ears are open to their prayer. But the face of the Lord is against those who do evil.' Now who will harm you if you are eager to do what is good? But even if you do suffer for doing what is right, you are blessed. Do not fear what they fear, and do not be intimidated, but in your hearts sanctify Christ as Lord. Always be ready to make your defence to anyone who demands from you an account of the hope that is in you; yet do it with gentleness and reverence. Keep your conscience clear, so that, when you are maligned, those who abuse you for your good conduct in Christ may be put to shame. For it is better to suffer for doing good, if suffering should be God's will, than to suffer for doing evil. For Christ also suffered for sins once for all, the righteous for the unrighteous, in order to bring you to God. He was put to death in the flesh, but made alive in the spirit. (1 Peter 3: 8–18)

## Song

O gladsome light, O grace
Of God the Father's face,
The eternal splendour wearing;
Celestial, holy blest,
Our Saviour Jesus Christ,
Joyful in thine appearing.

Now ere day fadeth quite,
We see the evening light,
Our wonted hymn outpouring;
Father of might unknown,
Thee, his incarnate Son,
And Holy Spirit adoring.

To thee of right belongs
All praise of holy songs,
O Son of God, lifegiver;
Thee, therefore, O Most High,
The world doth glorify,
And shall exalt for ever.

'Evening Prayer', *Alternative Service Book*

## Prayer

Holy Spirit of joy and of peace, come to us this evening. Bring us your calm; fill us with compassion for others so that all may be drawn to your heavenly light, Amen.

# LENT FRIDAYS

## MORNING PRAYER

### Greeting

I fled Him, down the nights and down the days;
I fled Him, down the arches of the years;
I fled Him, down the labyrinthine ways
Of my own mind; and in the midst of tears
I hid from Him, and under running laughter.

Francis Thompson, 1859–1907

The Lord is my rock, my fortress, and my deliverer, my God, my rock, in whom I take refuge, my shield and the horn of my salvation, my stronghold and my refuge, my saviour. (2 Samuel 22:2–3)

### Reflection

Jesus is our Saviour. During Lent we contemplate the saving mysteries of our redemption and renew our faith. We cling to the rock of salvation, safe in the knowledge that God wills our good. The whole of nature is caught into the dramatic action of God when he intervenes to draw us out of danger to a place of safety and blessing. We join with Moses in his song of triumphant praise.

### Reading

Then Moses and the Israelites sang this song to the Lord: 'I will sing to the Lord, for he has triumphed gloriously; horse and rider he has thrown into the sea. The Lord is my strength and my might, and he has become my salvation; this is my God, and I will praise him, my father's God, and I will exalt him. The Lord is a warrior; the Lord is his name. Pharaoh's chariots and his army he cast into the sea; his picked officers were sunk in the Red Sea. The floods covered them; they went down into the depths like a stone. Your right hand, O Lord, glorious in power – your right hand, O Lord, shattered the enemy. In the greatness of your majesty you overthrew your adversaries; you sent out your fury, it consumed them like stubble. At the blast of your nostrils the waters piled up, the floods stood up in a heap; the deeps congealed in the heart of the sea. The enemy said, "I will pursue, I will overtake, I will divide the spoil, my desire shall have its fill of them. I will draw my sword, my hand shall destroy them." You blew with your wind, the sea covered them; they sank like lead in the mighty waters. Who is like you, O Lord, among the gods? Who is like you, majestic in holiness, awesome in splendour, doing wonders? You stretched out your right hand, the earth swallowed them. In your steadfast love you led the people whom you redeemed; you guided them by your strength to your holy abode.' (Exodus 15:1–13)

## Song

Rock of ages, cleft for me,
Let me hide myself in thee;
Let the water and the blood,
From thy riven side which flowed,
Be of sin the double cure:
Cleanse me from its guilt and power.

Not the labours of my hands
Can fulfil thy law's demands:
Could my zeal no respite know,
Could my tears for ever flow,
All for sin could not atone:
Thou must save, and thou alone.

Nothing in my hand I bring:
Simply to thy cross I cling:
Naked, come to thee for dress:
Helpless, look to thee for grace:
Foul, I to the fountain fly:
Wash me, Saviour, or I die.

While I draw this fleeting breath,
When my eyes shall close in death,
When I soar through tracts unknown,

See thee on thy judgement throne:
Rock of ages, cleft for me,
Let me hide myself in thee.

Augustus Montague Toplady, 1740–78

## Prayer

'Wash me, Saviour, or I die.' Lord Jesus Christ, Saviour of our world, cleanse us from sin, bring us to grace, bring us to hope, bring us to glory. Inspire in us the desire to bring your grace and hope and glory into the lives of all we love, Amen.

❧

# EVENING PRAYER

## Greeting

I will sing a new song to you, O God; upon a ten-stringed harp I will play to you. (Psalm 144:9)

Bring your harps, and bring your incense,
sweep the string and pour the lay.

Job Hupton, 1762–1849

## Reflection

The Benedictus is one of the oldest of Christian prayers. When the birth of John the Baptist is announced to his father, he falls dumb, regaining his speech only when the child is born and he writes down the boy's name: John. Then Zechariah bursts into song and praises God for the gift of salvation. His son will be a precursor; Jesus is our Saviour.

## Reading

'Blessed be the Lord God of Israel, for he has looked favourably on his people and redeemed them. He has raised up a mighty saviour for us in the house of his servant David, as he spoke through the mouth of his holy prophets from of old, that we would be saved from our enemies and from the hand of all who hate us. Thus he has shown the mercy promised to our ancestors, and has remembered his holy covenant, the oath that he swore to our ancestor Abraham, to grant us that we, being rescued from the hands of our enemies, might serve him without fear, in holiness and righteousness before him all our days. And you, child, will be called the prophet of the Most High; for you will go before the Lord to prepare his ways, to give knowledge of salvation to his people by the forgiveness of their sins. By the tender mercy of our God, the dawn from on high will break upon us, to give light to those who sit in darkness and in the shadow of death, to guide our feet into the way of peace.' (Luke 1:68–79)

## Song

Soul of my Saviour, sanctify my breast,
Body of Christ, be thou my saving guest,
Blood of my Saviour, bathe me in thy tide,
Wash me with water flowing from thy side.

Strength and protection may thy passion be,
O blessed Jesus, hear and answer me;
Deep in thy wounds, Lord, hide and shelter me,
So shall I never, never part from thee.

Guard and defend me from the foe malign,
In death's dread moments make me only thine;
Call me and bid me come to thee on high
Where I may praise thee with thy saints for ay.

Latin, fourteenth century, tr. J. Hegarty SJ, d. 1834

## Prayer

Jesus is our Saviour. We pray tonight for the salvation of the world. Come, Lord Jesus, come to our needy world. Inspire in us the courage to work for change so that all may know that you are the true Saviour of our souls, Amen.

# LENT SATURDAYS

## MORNING PRAYER

### Greeting

Happy are those who live in your house, ever singing your praise. Happy are those whose strength is in you, in whose heart are the highways to Zion. As they go through the valley of Baca they make it a place of springs. (Psalm 84:4–6)

We have left undone those things which we ought to have done;
And we have done those things which we ought not to have done;
And there is no health in us.

'General Confession', *Book of Common Prayer*

### Reflection

Saturday is a day of rest, a sabbath when we sing the praise of God and remember that our only health lies in God and in the redemption Jesus won for us. The glory of God is our glory too because we are ransomed, healed, restored and forgiven. The saving work of Jesus is done, achieved, completed. We may lie down in safety and rise with Christ, giving thanks and praise to God, in the power of the Spirit.

### Reading

The twenty-four elders and the four living creatures fell down and worshipped God who is seated on the throne, saying, 'Amen. Hallelujah!' And from the throne came a voice saying, 'Praise our God, all you his servants, and all who fear him, small and great.' Then I heard what seemed to be the voice of a great multitude, like the sound of many waters and like the sound of mighty thunder-peals, crying out, 'Hallelujah! For the Lord our God the Almighty reigns. Let us rejoice and exult and give him the glory, for the marriage of the Lamb has come, and

his bride has made herself ready; to her it has been granted to
be clothed with fine linen, bright and pure' – for the fine linen
is the righteous deeds of the saints. And the angel said to me,
'Write this: Blessed are those who are invited to the marriage
supper of the Lamb.' And he said to me, 'These are true words
of God.' Then I fell down at his feet to worship him, but he said
to me, 'You must not do that! I am a fellow servant with you
and your comrades who hold the testimony of Jesus. Worship
God! For the testimony of Jesus is the spirit of prophecy.'
(Revelation 19:4–10)

## Song

Praise to the Holiest in the height,
And in the depth be praise;
In all his words most wonderful,
Most sure in all his ways.

O loving wisdom of our God!
When all was sin and shame,
A second Adam to the fight
And to the rescue came.

O wisest love! that flesh and blood,
Which did in Adam fail,
Should strive afresh against the foe,
Should strive and should prevail;

And that a higher gift than grace
Should flesh and blood refine,
God's presence and his very self,
And essence all-divine.

O generous love! that he, who smote
In man for man the foe,
The double agony in man
For man should undergo;

And in the garden secretly,
And on the cross on high,
Should teach his brethren, and inspire
To suffer and to die.

Praise to the Holiest in the height,
And in the depth be praise;
In all his words most wonderful,
Most sure in all his ways.

John Henry Newman, 1801–90

## Prayer

'Worship God! For the testimony of Jesus is the spirit of prophecy.'
Today we worship God by singing the divine praises. 'Praise to the
Holiest in the height.' Loving Lord, God of the living and the dead,
we praise you for your glory and majesty; call us to the marriage
feast of the Lamb, Amen.

# EVENING PRAYER

## Greeting

But when Christ came as a high priest of the good things that
have come, then through the greater and perfect tent (not made
with hands, that is, not of this creation), he entered once for all
into the Holy Place, not with the blood of goats and calves, but
with his own blood, thus obtaining eternal redemption.
(Hebrews 9:11–12)

*O felix culpa, quae talem ac tantum meruit habere Redemptorem.*
O happy fault, which has earned the possession of such, and so
great a Redeemer.

'*Exsultet* on Holy Saturday', *Roman Missal*

## Reflection

During Lent we pray for the strengthening of our faith. We pray to
understand the mysteries of our redemption so that we can assent to
the work that has been done for us and in us by the passion and
resurrection of Jesus. Our patience is rewarded by joy as our sins
are forgiven. Every Saturday night mirrors the night of waiting when
Jesus went down among the dead and harrowed hell, bringing the
souls of the faithful departed to the fullness of the promise.

## Reading

May you be made strong with all the strength that comes from his glorious power, and may you be prepared to endure everything with patience, while joyfully giving thanks to the Father, who has enabled you to share in the inheritance of the saints in the light. He has rescued us from the power of darkness and transferred us into the kingdom of his beloved Son, in whom we have redemption, the forgiveness of sins. He is the image of the invisible God, the firstborn of all creation; for in him all things in heaven and on earth were created, things visible and invisible, whether thrones or dominions or rulers or powers – all things have been created through him and for him. He himself is before all things, and in him all things hold together. He is the head of the body, the church; he is the beginning, the firstborn from the dead, so that he might come to have first place in everything. For in him all the fullness of God was pleased to dwell, and through him God was pleased to reconcile to himself all things, whether on earth or in heaven, by making peace through the blood of his cross. And you who were once estranged and hostile in mind, doing evil deeds, he has now reconciled in his fleshly body through death, so as to present you holy and blameless and irreproachable before him – provided that you continue securely established and steadfast in the faith, without shifting from the hope promised by the gospel that you heard, which has been proclaimed to every creature under heaven. (Colossians 1:13–23)

## Song

Guide me, O Thou great Jehovah,
Pilgrim through this barren land;
I am weak, but thou art mighty,
Hold me with thy powerful hand;
Bread of heaven,
Feed me till I want no more.

Open now, the crystal fountain,
Whence the healing stream doth flow;
Let the fiery, cloudy pillar
Lead me all my journey through:
Strong deliverer,
Be Thou still my strength and shield.

When I tread the verge of Jordan,
Bid my anxious fears subside;
Death of death and hell's destruction;
Land me safe on Canaan's side:
Songs of praises
I will ever give to thee.

William Williams, 1717–91

## Prayer

We pray for the fullness of the life of faith; we pray for God's kingdom to come. Heavenly Father, who called Jesus out of death into life by the power of the Holy Spirit, call us too; strengthen our faith and give us your patience and your joy, Amen.

# EASTER SUNDAY

## MORNING PRAYER

### Greeting

The Lord is my strength and my might; he has become my salvation. There are glad songs of victory in the tents of the righteous: I shall not die, but I shall live, and recount the deeds of the Lord. (Psalm 118:14–15, 17)

I heard a voice which said, 'There is one, even Christ Jesus, that can speak to thy condition', and when I heard it, my heart did leap for joy.

George Fox, 1624–91

### Reflection

Christ, our Lord, is risen in glory. Our celebration of Easter begins as we listen to the good news that Jesus is risen from the dead. With Mary Magdalene, we venture forth in the cool light of early morning and find that the tomb is empty. With Peter and John we begin to believe the unbelievable as we gaze at the evidence. Our relationship with our Risen Lord is strengthened as the dawn light breaks on the empty tomb.

### Reading

Early on the first day of the week, while it was still dark, Mary Magdalene came to the tomb and saw that the stone had been removed from the tomb. So she ran and went to Simon Peter and the other disciple, the one whom Jesus loved, and said to them, 'They have taken the Lord out of the tomb, and we do not know where they have laid him.' Then Peter and the other disciple set out and went toward the tomb. The two were running together, but the other disciple outran Peter and reached the tomb first. He bent down to look in and saw the linen wrappings lying there, but he did not go in. Then Simon Peter came, following him, and went into the tomb. He saw the linen wrappings lying there, and the cloth that had been on Jesus' head, not lying with the linen wrappings but rolled up in a place by itself. Then the other disciple, who reached the tomb first, also went in, and he saw and believed; for as yet they did not understand the scripture, that he must rise from the dead. Then the disciples returned to their homes. (John 20:1–10)

## Song

This joyful Eastertide,
away with sin and sorrow!
My love, the crucified,
hath sprung to life this morrow.
*Had Christ, that once was slain,*
*ne'er burst his three-day prison,*
*our faith had been in vain:*
*but now hath Christ arisen,*
*arisen, arisen, arisen.*

My flesh in hope shall rest,
and for a season slumber:
till trump from east to west
shall wake the dead in number.
*Had Christ, that once was slain . . .*

Death's flood hath lost his chill,
since Jesus crossed the river:
lover of souls, from ill
my passing soul deliver.
*Had Christ, that once was slain . . .*

G. R. Woodward, 1848–1934

## Prayer

Lord Jesus Christ, our risen Saviour, bring us to your empty tomb and fill us with your love. Raise our eyes to heaven where you live and reign in glory forever, Amen.

❧

# EVENING PRAYER

## Greeting

Men fear death as children fear to go in the dark; and as that
natural fear in children is increased with tales, so is the other.

Francis Bacon, 1561–1626

Jacob left Beer-sheba and went towards Haran. He came to a
certain place and stayed there for the night, because the sun
had set. Taking one of the stones of the place, he put it under
his head and lay down in that place. And he dreamed that there
was a ladder set up on the earth, the top of it reaching to heaven;
and the angels of God were ascending and descending on it.
(Genesis 28:10–12)

## Reflection

'The last enemy to be destroyed is death.' When Jesus is raised from
the dead, death loses its power over us. We can face our own future
with confidence and hope because the work of our redemption is
done. Angels ascend and descend into our world. We can lie down
to sleep without fear, confident that our lives are held within the life
of God.

## Reading

Now if Christ is proclaimed as raised from the dead, how can
some of you say there is no resurrection of the dead? If there is
no resurrection of the dead, then Christ has not been raised;
and if Christ has not been raised, then our proclamation has
been in vain and your faith has been in vain. We are even found
to be misrepresenting God, because we testified of God that he
raised Christ – whom he did not raise if it is true that the dead
are not raised. For if the dead are not raised, then Christ has
not been raised. If Christ has not been raised, your faith is futile
and you are still in your sins. Then those also who have died in
Christ have perished. If for this life only we have hoped in
Christ, we are of all people most to be pitied. But in fact Christ
has been raised from the dead, the first fruits of those who have
died. For since death came through a human being, the
resurrection of the dead has also come through a human being;

for as all die in Adam, so all will be made alive in Christ. But each in his own order: Christ the first fruits, then at his coming those who belong to Christ. Then comes the end, when he hands over the kingdom to God the Father, after he has destroyed every ruler and every authority and power. For he must reign until he has put all his enemies under his feet. The last enemy to be destroyed is death. (1 Corinthians 15:12–26)

## Song

Thine be the glory, risen, conquering Son,
endless is the victory thou o'er death hast won;
angels in bright raiment rolled the stone away,
kept the folded grave-clothes where thy body lay.
*Thine be the glory, risen, conquering Son,*
*endless is the victory thou o'er death hast won.*

Lo, Jesus meets us, risen from the tomb;
lovingly he greets us, scatters fear and gloom;
let the church with gladness hymns of triumph sing,
for her Lord now liveth, death hath lost its sting:
*Thine be the glory, risen, conquering Son . . .*

No more we doubt thee, glorious prince of life;
life is nought without thee: aid us in our strife;
make us more than conquerors through thy deathless love;
bring us safe through Jordan to thy home above:
*Thine be the glory, risen, conquering Son . . .*

E. L. Budry, 1854–1932

## Prayer

We pray in confidence, knowing that our Saviour is risen: come to us now, Lord; comfort us with the certainty that death has lost its power over us; call us to sleep in your name, Amen.

# EASTER MONDAY

## MORNING PRAYER

### Greeting

Because the Holy Ghost over the bent
World broods with warm breast and with ah!
Bright wings.

Gerard Manley Hopkins, 1844–89

'And now, O Lord, what do I wait for? My hope is in you.
Deliver me from all my transgressions.' (Psalm 39:7–8)

### Reflection

Jesus alone is the source of our hope. Jesus alone knows us through
and through and offers us true hope by delivering us from our sins
and reversing the judgement which was placed upon us in the first
garden, the Garden of Eden. With Mary, we come to the garden of
the resurrection. With her we seek the risen Lord and find him where
we least expect, in the known and the familiar. With her we go out
and proclaim the news that Jesus is risen from the dead and that our
salvation is bound up in the mysteries which we celebrate this week.

### Reading

But Mary stood weeping outside the tomb. As she wept, she
bent over to look into the tomb; and she saw two angels in
white, sitting where the body of Jesus had been lying, one at
the head and the other at the feet. They said to her, 'Woman,
why are you weeping?' She said to them, 'They have taken away
my Lord, and I do not know where they have laid him.' When
she had said this, she turned around and saw Jesus standing
there, but she did not know that it was Jesus. Jesus said to her,
'Woman, why are you weeping? Whom are you looking for?'
Supposing him to be the gardener, she said to him, 'Sir, if you

have carried him away, tell me where you have laid him, and I will take him away.' Jesus said to her, 'Mary!' She turned and said to him in Hebrew, 'Rabbouni!' (which means Teacher). Jesus said to her, 'Do not hold on to me, because I have not yet ascended to the Father. But go to my brothers and say to them, "I am ascending to my Father and your Father, to my God and your God." ' Mary Magdalene went and announced to the disciples, 'I have seen the Lord'; and she told them that he had said these things to her. (John 20:11–18)

## Song

Christ the Lord is risen again!
Christ hath broken every chain!
Hark! Angelic voices cry,
singing evermore on high,
Alleluia!

He who gave for us his life,
who for us endured the strife,
is our Paschal lamb today;
we too sing for joy, and say
Alleluia!

He who bore all pain and loss
comfortless upon the cross,
lives in glory now on high,
pleads for us, and hears our cry:
Alleluia!

He whose path no records tell,
who descended into hell,
who the strong man armed hath bound,
now in highest heaven is crowned.
Alleluia!

He who slumbered in the grave
is exalted now to save;
now through Christendom it rings
that the lamb is King of kings.
Alleluia!

Now he bids us tell abroad
how the lost may be restored,
how the penitent forgiven,
how we too may enter heaven.
Alleluia!

Thou, our Paschal lamb indeed,
Christ, thy ransomed people feed;
take our sins and guilt away,
let us sing by night and day,
Alleluia!

M. Weisse, 1480–1534, tr. Catherine Winkworth, 1829–78

## Prayer

Christ our Paschal lamb is risen from the dead. We pray for true
hope, confident that Jesus secures our forgiveness. Beloved Lord,
receive our song of praise, bring us to the garden of your holy
resurrection, Amen.

# EVENING PRAYER

## Greeting

Stand up! Stand up for Jesus, Ye soldiers of the Cross!
George Duffield, 1818–88

If, because of the one man's trespass, death exercised dominion
through that one, much more surely will those who receive the
abundance of grace and the free gift of righteousness exercise
dominion in life through the one man, Jesus Christ. (Romans
5:17)

## Reflection

We ordinarily think about the resurrection from the perspective of
the first followers of Jesus, those who had watched him die and
thought that they had lost him forever. This evening we think about
the resurrection from the perspective of God, who receives his Son
in glory through the power of the Holy Spirit and who gives him
dominion over our hearts and minds and souls.

## Reading

As I watched in the night visions, I saw one like a human being coming with the clouds of heaven. And he came to the Ancient One and was presented before him. To him was given dominion and glory and kingship, that all peoples, nations, and languages should serve him. His dominion is an everlasting dominion that shall not pass away, and his kingship is one that shall never be destroyed. (Daniel 7:13–14)

## Song

Ye choirs of new Jerusalem,
your sweetest notes employ,
the Paschal victory to hymn
in strains of holy joy.

How Judah's lion burst his chains,
and crushed the serpent's head;
and brought with him, from death's domains,
the long-imprisoned dead.

From hell's devouring jaws the prey
alone our leader bore;
his ransomed hosts pursue their way
where he hath gone before.

Triumphant in his glory now
his sceptre ruleth all,
earth, heaven, and hell before him bow,
and at his footstool fall.

While joyful thus his praise we sing,
his mercy we implore,
into his palace bright to bring
and keep us evermore.

All glory to the Father be,
all glory to the Son,
all glory, Holy Ghost, to thee,
while endless ages run. Alleluya! Amen.

> St Fulbert of Chartres, eleventh century,
> tr. Robert Campbell, 1814–68

# Prayer

The mystery of salvation is made complete when Jesus is received into heaven in glory. Heavenly Father who opened the gates of heaven to Jesus, your Son, made like us and one of us, open the gates of our faith to receive him and to accept his dominion over our lives, Amen.

# EASTER TUESDAY

## MORNING PRAYER

### Greeting

God tempers the wind . . . to the shorn lamb.

Laurence Sterne, 1713–68

Know that the Lord is God. It is he that made us, and we are his; we are his people, and the sheep of his pasture. Enter his gates with thanksgiving, and his courts with praise. Give thanks to him, bless his name. (Psalm 100:3–4)

### Reflection

Jesus, the risen shepherd of his sheep, gathers in his own. Some of the earliest images of the risen Christ show him carrying sheep into the fold of salvation. We go with him there, giving thanks and blessing his name. The promise of the new covenant is secured for us when the sheep are gathered in and the bread and new wine of the kingdom become our food and drink.

### Reading

While they were eating, he took a loaf of bread, and after blessing it he broke it, gave it to them, and said, 'Take; this is my body.' Then he took a cup, and after giving thanks he gave it to them, and all of them drank from it. He said to them, 'This is my blood of the covenant, which is poured out for many. Truly I tell you, I will never again drink of the fruit of the vine until that day when I drink it new in the kingdom of God.' When they had sung the hymn, they went out to the Mount of Olives. And Jesus said to them, 'You will all become deserters; for it is written, "I will strike the shepherd, and the sheep will be scattered." But after I am raised up, I will go before you to Galilee.' (Mark 14:22–8)

## Song

The God of love my shepherd is,
and he that doth me feed;
while he is mine and I am his,
what can I want or need?

He leads me to the tender grass,
where I both feed and rest;
then to the streams that gently pass:
in both I have the best.

Or if I stray, he doth convert,
and bring my mind in frame,
and all this not for my desert,
but for his holy name.

Yea, in death's shady black abode
well may I walk, not fear;
for thou art with me, and thy rod
to guide, thy staff to bear.

Surely thy sweet and wondrous love
shall measure all my days;
and, as it never shall remove,
so neither shall my praise.

George Herbert, 1593–1632

## Prayer

'Give us this day our daily bread.' Renew the life of the kingdom
within us and call us to your sheepfold, for ever and ever, Amen.

# EVENING PRAYER

## Greeting

Is it so small a thing
To have enjoy'd the sun,
To have liv'd light in the spring,
To have lov'd, to have thought, to have done?

Matthew Arnold, 1822–88

On that day there shall not be either cold or frost. And there shall be continuous day (it is known to the Lord), not day and not night, for at evening time there shall be light. (Zechariah 14:6–7)

## Reflection

Jesus walks with us on the road to our own particular Emmaus. He takes the risk of walking with us, even if we are going away from the holy city of peace and the fulfilment of God's promise to a place where we feel we are without hope and that the day is over. He stays with us until we recognise him and then calls us to return with him to Jerusalem, where we are to tell our friends that our faith is renewed and that, even at evening time, there is light and hope and joy. Christ is risen from the dead, Alleluia!

## Reading

As they came near the village to which they were going, he walked ahead as if he were going on. But they urged him strongly, saying, 'Stay with us, because it is almost evening and the day is now nearly over.' So he went in to stay with them. When he was at the table with them, he took bread, blessed and broke it, and gave it to them. Then their eyes were opened, and they recognized him; and he vanished from their sight. They said to each other, 'Were not our hearts burning within us while he was talking to us on the road, while he was opening the scriptures to us?' That same hour they got up and returned to Jerusalem; and they found the eleven and their companions gathered together. They were saying, 'The Lord has risen indeed, and he has appeared to Simon!' Then they told what had happened on the road, and how he had been made known to them in the breaking of the bread. (Luke 24:28–35)

## Song

Alleluia! Sing to Jesus!
His the sceptre, his the throne;
alleluia! His the triumph,
his the victory alone:
hark! The songs of peaceful Sion
thunder like a mighty flood;
Jesus out of every nation
hath redeemed us by his blood.

Alleluia! Not as orphans
are we left in sorrow now;
alleluia! He is near us,
faith believes, nor questions how:
though the cloud from sight received him,
when the forty days were o'er,
shall our hearts forget his promise,
'I am with you evermore'?

Alleluia! Bread of angels,
thou on earth our food, our stay;
alleluia! Here the sinful
flee to thee from day to day:
intercessor, friend of sinners,
earth's Redeemer, plead for me,
where the songs of all the sinless
sweep across the crystal sea.

Alleluia! King eternal,
thee the Lord of Lords we own;
alleluia! Born of Mary,
earth thy footstool, heaven thy throne:
thou within the veil hast entered,
robed in flesh, our great high priest;
thou on earth both priest and victim
in the Eucharistic feast.

W. Chatterton Dix, 1837–98

## Prayer

Come to us, Lord. Greet us now. Renew us in the breaking of the
bread, in the feast of love and hope and life which you offer us today
and every day; give us your peace, Amen.

# EASTER WEDNESDAY

## MORNING PRAYER

### Greeting

We are writing these things so that our joy may be complete. (1 John 1:4)

How sweet the Name of Jesus sounds
In a believer's ear!
It soothes his sorrows, heals his wounds,
And drives away his fear.
It makes the wounded spirit whole,
And calms the troubled breast;
'Tis manna to the hungry soul,
And to the weary rest.

John Newton, 1725–1807

### Reflection

Salvation is given to us in the name of Jesus, so we repeat the holy name of Jesus over and over again, for the salvation of our souls. We are offered joy, a new birth and a living hope. 'Hail the day that sees him rise', we pray, confident that we are made for the glory and praise of God and that when we praise God we fulfil a unique destiny.

### Reading

Blessed be the God and Father of our Lord Jesus Christ! By his great mercy he has given us a new birth into a living hope through the resurrection of Jesus Christ from the dead, and into an inheritance that is imperishable, undefiled, and unfading, kept in heaven for you, who are being protected by the power of God through faith for a salvation ready to be revealed in the last time. In this you rejoice, even if now for a little while you have had to suffer various trials, so that the genuineness of your faith – being more precious than gold that, though perishable, is tested by fire – may be found to result in praise and glory and honour when Jesus Christ is revealed. Although you have not seen him, you love him; and even though you do not see him now, you believe in him and rejoice with an indescribable and glorious joy, for you are receiving the outcome of your faith, the salvation of your souls. (1 Peter 1:3–9)

## Song

Hail the day that sees him rise, Alleluia!
To his throne above the skies; Alleluia!
Christ, the lamb for sinners given, Alleluia!
Enters now the highest heaven. Alleluia!

There for him high triumph waits; Alleluia!
Lift your heads, eternal gates! Alleluia!
He hath conquered death and sin; Alleluia!
Take the King of glory in! Alleluia!

Lo, the heaven its Lord receives, Alleluia!
Yet he loves the earth he leaves; Alleluia!
Though returning to his throne, Alleluia!
Still he calls mankind his own. Alleluia!

See! He lifts his hands above; Alleluia!
See! He shows the prints of love; Alleluia!
Hark! His gracious lips bestow, Alleluia!
Blessings on his Church below. Alleluia!

Still for us he intercedes, Alleluia!
His prevailing death he pleads; Alleluia!
Near himself prepares our place, Alleluia!
He the first-fruits of our race. Alleluia!

Lord, though parted from our sight, Alleluia!
Far above the starry height, Alleluia!
Grant our hearts may thither rise, Alleluia!
Seeking thee above the skies. Alleluia!

     Charles Wesley, 1707–88, and T. Cotterill, 1779–1823

## Prayer

Lord Jesus Christ, source of our joy and our hope, intercede for us now. Heal our wounds, drive away our fears, Amen.

# EVENING PRAYER

## Greeting

Weary with toil, I haste me to my bed,
The dear repose for limbs with travel tired;
But then begins a journey in my head
To work my mind when body's work's expired.

William Shakespeare, 1564–1616

He said to them, 'Take nothing for your journey, no staff, nor bag, nor bread, nor money – not even an extra tunic.' (Luke 9:3)

## Reflection

As night falls we rest in the sure hope that Jesus Christ is our Saviour and that we need have no fear. In him all is light and there is no darkness. The whole world is redeemed in the redeeming work of the Saviour and so we have hope. A new light is made known to us as he rises from the dead. We let our minds roam over the day and its works, confident that our sins are forgiven and that we are known and loved through and through.

## Reading

This is the message we have heard from him and proclaim to you, that God is light and in him there is no darkness at all. If we say that we have fellowship with him while we are walking in darkness, we lie and do not do what is true; but if we walk in the light as he himself is in the light, we have fellowship with one another, and the blood of Jesus his Son cleanses us from all sin. If we say that we have no sin, we deceive ourselves, and the truth is not in us. If we confess our sins, he who is faithful and just will forgive us our sins and cleanse us from all unrighteousness. If we say that we have not sinned, we make him a liar, and his word is not in us. My little children, I am writing these things to you so that you may not sin. But if anyone does sin, we have an advocate with the Father, Jesus Christ the righteous; and he is the atoning sacrifice for our sins, and not for ours only but also for the sins of the whole world. (1 John 1:5–2:2)

## Song

It is a thing most wonderful,
almost too wonderful to be,
that God's own Son should come from heaven,
and die to save a child like me.

And yet I know that it is true:
he chose a poor and humble lot,
and wept and toiled and mourned and died
for love of those who loved him not.

I cannot tell how he could love,
a child so weak and full of sin;
his love must be most wonderful,
if he could die my love to win.

I sometimes think about the cross,
and shut my eyes, and try to see
the cruel nails and crown of thorns,
and Jesus crucified for me.

But even could I see him die,
I could but see a little part
of that great love which, like a fire,
is always burning in his heart.

It is most wonderful to know
his love for me so free and sure;
but 'tis more wonderful to see
my love for him so faint and poor.

And yet I want to love thee, Lord!
O light the flame within my heart,
and I will love thee more and more,
until I see thee as thou art.

W. Walsham How, 1823–97

## Prayer

Come into our lives, Lord Jesus. Be our light and take away the darkness of our sin and fear. Enlighten our hearts and our minds; fill our world with your light, Amen.

# EASTER THURSDAY

## MORNING PRAYER

### Greeting

As kingfishers catch fire, dragonflies draw flame;
As tumbled over rim in roundy wells
Stones ring.

Gerard Manley Hopkins, 1844–89

But now in Christ Jesus you who once were far off have been brought near by the blood of Christ. For he is our peace; in his flesh he has made both groups into one and has broken down the dividing wall, that is, the hostility between us. (Ephesians 2:13–14)

### Reflection

The resurrection of Jesus offers us spiritual renewal. We are to be transformed by the renewal of our minds. So what does this mean? Transformation is about growth and the possibility of change. The gospel call does not allow us to stand still. Rather it asks us to care for other people as a sign that we are transformed. In this way we are to present our bodies as a living sacrifice, to show our belief in the power of God's call to us.

### Reading

O the depth of the riches and wisdom and knowledge of God! How unsearchable are his judgements and how inscrutable his ways! 'For who has known the mind of the Lord? Or who has been his counsellor?' 'Or who has given a gift to him, to receive a gift in return?' For from him and through him and to him are all things. To him be the glory forever. Amen. I appeal to you therefore, brothers and sisters, by the mercies of God, to present your bodies as a living sacrifice, holy and acceptable to God, which is your spiritual worship. Do not be conformed to this world, but be transformed by the renewing of your minds, so that you may discern what is the will of God – what is good and acceptable and perfect. (Romans 11:33–12:2)

## Song

At the name of Jesus
every knee shall bow,
every tongue confess him
King of glory now.
'Tis the Father's pleasure
we should call him Lord,
who from the beginning
was the mighty Word.

At his voice creation
sprang at once to sight,
all the angel faces,
all the hosts of light,
thrones and dominations,
stars upon their way,
all the heavenly orders,
in their great array.

Humbled for a season,
to receive a name
from the lips of sinners
unto whom he came,
faithfully he bore it
spotless to the last,
brought it back victorious,
when from death he passed:

Bore it up triumphant
with its human light,
through all ranks of creatures,
to the central height,
to the throne of Godhead,
to the Father's breast;
filled it with the glory
of that perfect rest.

Caroline M. Noel, 1817–77

## Prayer

Lord of heaven and earth, give us the grace to serve you in confidence by serving others. Be our security and our life, Amen.

❧

# EVENING PRAYER

## Greeting

There we leave you, in that blessed dependency, to hang upon
him that hangs upon the Cross, there bathe in his tears, there
suck at his wounds, and lie down in peace in his grave, till he
vouchsafe you a resurrection, and an ascension into that
Kingdom, which he hath prepared for you, with the inestimable
price of his incorruptible blood. Amen.

John Donne, 1572–1631

He has rescued us from the power of darkness and transferred
us into the kingdom of his beloved Son, in whom we have
redemption, the forgiveness of sins. (Colossians 1:13–14)

## Reflection

'Jesus is the Messiah', so we are able to come to him with all our
hopes and all our doubts. Faith is not the same as certainty, so in the
life of faith we are able to express our doubts. With Thomas, we
kneel at the feet of our Saviour and we say, 'My Lord and my God'.

## Reading

But Thomas (who was called the Twin), one of the twelve, was
not with them when Jesus came. So the other disciples told
him, 'We have seen the Lord.' But he said to them, 'Unless I see
the mark of the nails in his hands, and put my finger in the
mark of the nails and my hand in his side, I will not believe.' A
week later his disciples were again in the house, and Thomas
was with them. Although the doors were shut, Jesus came and
stood among them and said, 'Peace be with you.' Then he said
to Thomas, 'Put your finger here and see my hands. Reach out
your hand and put it in my side. Do not doubt but believe.'
Thomas answered him, 'My Lord and my God!' Jesus said to
him, 'Have you believed because you have seen me? Blessed
are those who have not seen and yet have come to believe.'

Now Jesus did many other signs in the presence of his disciples,
which are not written in this book. But these are written so that
you may come to believe that Jesus is the Messiah, the Son of
God, and that through believing you may have life in his name.
(John 20:24–31)

## Song

O sons and daughters, let us sing!
The king of heaven, the glorious king,
o'er death today rose triumphing.
Alleluia!

That Easter morn, at break of day,
the faithful women went their way
to seek the tomb where Jesus lay.
Alleluia!

An angel clad in white they see,
who sat, and spake unto the three,
'Your Lord doth go to Galilee.'
Alleluia!

That night the apostles met in fear;
amidst them came their Lord most dear,
and said, 'My peace be on all here.'
Alleluia!

When Thomas first the tidings heard,
how they had seen the risen Lord,
he doubted the disciples' word.
Alleluia!

'My pierced side, O Thomas, see;
my hands, my feet I show to thee;
not faithless, but believing be.'
Alleluia!

No longer Thomas then denied;
he saw the feet, the hands, the side;
'Thou art my Lord and God,' he cried.
Alleluia!

How blest are they who have not seen,
and yet whose faith hath constant been!
For they eternal life shall win.
Alleluia!

On this most holy day of days,
to God your hearts and voices raise
in laud and jubilee and praise.
Alleluia!

J. Tisserand, d. 1914, tr. J. M. Neale, 1818–66

## Prayer

'My Lord and my God.' We pray tonight for Jesus to stand at the
door of our lives and knock. With Thomas we say, 'My Lord and my
God', Amen.

# EASTER FRIDAY

## MORNING PRAYER

### Greeting

> At the round earth's imagined corners, blow
> Your trumpets, Angels, and arise, arise
> From death, you numberless infinities
> Of souls.

John Donne, 1572–1631

> In him we have redemption through his blood, the forgiveness of our trespasses, according to the riches of his grace that he lavished on us. (Ephesians 1:7–8)

### Reflection

Jesus is the fulfilment of the promise. Because the Spirit of the Lord is upon him, he brings good news to all. The whole of creation rejoices when the Lord's favour is made known to us. This means that there is hope for the poor and the weak, for those who are in a prison of pain and suffering, for all who are oppressed by the circumstances of their daily lives. The life of faith is meant to make a difference to how we live, so that selflessness lies at the heart of the gospel call.

### Reading

> When he came to Nazareth, where he had been brought up, he went to the synagogue on the sabbath day, as was his custom. He stood up to read, and the scroll of the prophet Isaiah was given to him. He unrolled the scroll and found the place where it was written: 'The Spirit of the Lord is upon me, because he has anointed me to bring good news to the poor. He has sent me to proclaim release to the captives and recovery of sight to the blind, to let the oppressed go free, to proclaim the year of the

Lord's favour.' And he rolled up the scroll, gave it back to the
attendant, and sat down. The eyes of all in the synagogue were
fixed on him. Then he began to say to them, 'Today this scripture
has been fulfilled in your hearing.' (Luke 4:16–21)

## Song

O for a thousand tongues to sing
my dear Redeemer's praise,
the glories of my God and King,
the triumph of his grace!

Jesus – the name that charms our fears,
that bids our sorrows cease;
'tis music in the sinner's ears,
'tis life, and health, and peace.

He breaks the power of cancelled sin,
he sets the prisoner free;
his blood can make the foulest clean;
his blood availed for me.

He speaks; and, listening to his voice,
new life the dead receive,
the mournful broken hearts rejoice,
the humble poor believe.

Hear him, ye deaf; his praise, ye dumb,
your loosened tongues employ;
ye blind, behold your Saviour come;
and leap, ye lame, for joy!

My gracious Master and my God,
assist me to proclaim
and spread through all the earth abroad
the honours of thy name.

Charles Wesley, 1707–88

## Prayer

Lord Jesus Christ, hope of the living and of all who seek for grace,
come to us now, change our lives and call us to your service, Amen.

# EVENING PRAYER

## Greeting

We bless thee for our creation, preservation, and all the blessings of this life; but above all, for thine inestimable love in the redemption of the world by our Lord Jesus Christ; for the means of grace, and for the hope of glory.

*Book of Common Prayer*

The Lord is my light and my salvation; whom shall I fear? The Lord is the stronghold of my life; of whom shall I be afraid? (Psalm 27:1)

## Reflection

Paul writes to the servants of God in the early Christian community, encouraging them to think about the new gift of God which is given to them. With the resurrection of Jesus everything is changed. So the old rules about circumcision or dietary laws no longer obtain. Instead we are marked with the cross of Christ which sets us free.

## Reading

See what large letters I make when I am writing in my own hand! It is those who want to make a good showing in the flesh that try to compel you to be circumcised – only that they may not be persecuted for the cross of Christ. Even the circumcised do not themselves obey the law, but they want you to be circumcised so that they may boast about your flesh. May I never boast of anything except the cross of our Lord Jesus Christ, by which the world has been crucified to me, and I to the world. For neither circumcision nor uncircumcision is anything; but a new creation is everything! As for those who will follow this rule – peace be upon them, and mercy, and upon the Israel of God. From now on, let no one make trouble for me; for I carry the marks of Jesus branded on my body. May the grace of our Lord Jesus Christ be with your spirit, brothers and sisters. Amen. (Galatians 6:11–18)

# Song

The head that once was crowned with thorns
is crowned with glory now,
a royal diadem adorns
the mighty victor's brow.

The highest place that heaven affords
is his, is his by right;
the King of kings, and Lord of lords,
and heaven's eternal light.

The joy of all who dwell above,
the joy of all below,
to whom he demonstrates his love,
and grants his name to know.

To them the cross with all its shame,
with all its grace is given;
their name, an everlasting name,
their joy, the joy of heaven.

They suffer with their Lord below,
they reign with him above;
their profit and their joy to know
the mystery of his love.

The cross he bore is life and health,
though shame and death to him;
his people's hope, his people's wealth,
their everlasting theme.

T. Kelly, 1769–1855

# Prayer

God our Father, source of our life and our very being; mark our
hearts with the life of Christ; mark our souls with the word of life,
Amen.

# EASTER SATURDAY

## MORNING PRAYER

### Greeting
More and more thyself display,
shining to the perfect day.

Charles Wesley, 1707–88

The Lord lives! Blessed be my rock, and exalted be my God, the rock of my salvation. (2 Samuel 22:47)

### Reflection
The life of faith takes us to the lakeside with Peter and the other apostles; we wait there for the Lord to join us and we listen to his question: 'You have no fish, have you?' Ask him now to come to you in your need. Listen to the beloved disciple as he says to you, 'It is the Lord'. Find the Lord where he is waiting for you and receive the gift of new life which he offers to you.

### Reading
Simon Peter said to them, 'I am going fishing.' They said to him, 'We will go with you.' They went out and got into the boat, but that night they caught nothing. Just after daybreak, Jesus stood on the beach; but the disciples did not know that it was Jesus. Jesus said to them, 'Children, you have no fish, have you?' They answered him, 'No.' He said to them, 'Cast the net to the right side of the boat, and you will find some.' So they cast it, and now they were not able to haul it in because there were so many fish. That disciple whom Jesus loved said to Peter, 'It is the Lord!' When Simon Peter heard that it was the Lord, he put on some clothes, for he was naked, and jumped into the sea. But the other disciples came in the boat, dragging the net full of fish, for they were not far from the land, only about a

hundred yards off. When they had gone ashore, they saw a charcoal fire there, with fish on it, and bread. Jesus said to them, 'Bring some of the fish that you have just caught.' So Simon Peter went aboard and hauled the net ashore, full of large fish, a hundred and fifty-three of them; and though there were so many, the net was not torn. Jesus said to them, 'Come and have breakfast.' Now none of the disciples dared to ask him, 'Who are you?' because they knew it was the Lord. Jesus came and took the bread and gave it to them, and did the same with the fish. This was now the third time that Jesus appeared to the disciples after he was raised from the dead. (John 21:3–14)

## Song

Jesus Christ is risen today, Alleluia!
Our triumphant holy day, Alleluia!
Who did once, upon the cross, Alleluia!
Suffer to redeem our loss. Alleluia!

Hymns of praise then let us sing, Alleluia!
Unto Christ, our heavenly King, Alleluia!
Who endured the cross and grave, Alleluia!
Sinners to redeem and save. Alleluia!

But the pains that he endured, Alleluia!
Our salvation have procured; Alleluia!
Now above the sky he's King, Alleluia!
Where the angels ever sing. Alleluia!

Based on a fourteenth-century hymn, *Lyra Davidica*

## Prayer

We pray to the Risen Lord as he comes to us and offers us food by the lakeside. Bless us, O Lord, bless our hopes and fears; bless us in our need. Help us to recognise you in the breaking of bread, Amen.

❧

# EVENING PRAYER

## Greeting

> Jesus shall reign where'er the sun
> Does his successive journeys run;
> His Kingdom stretch from shore to shore,
> Till moons shall wax and wane no more ...
> Blessings abound where'er He reigns;
> The prisoner leaps to lose his chains.

Isaac Watts, 1674–1748

'I wait for your salvation, O Lord.' (Genesis 49:18)

## Reflection

Jesus died for our salvation; Jesus rose from the dead for our salvation. Our lives are founded and moulded on his, so that the pattern of sacrificial love which he models for us becomes the pattern of our lives. We want to be identified with his work and to do his will; we want to turn to God in love and to find our fulfilment in him. So tonight, as we reflect again on the saving mysteries of our salvation, we enter more deeply into the heart of the mystery of God's love for us, made known in Jesus, our Saviour.

## Reading

> What then are we to say? Should we continue in sin in order that grace may abound? By no means! How can we who died to sin go on living in it? Do you not know that all of us who have been baptised into Christ Jesus were baptised into his death? Therefore we have been buried with him by baptism into death, so that, just as Christ was raised from the dead by the glory of the Father, so we too might walk in newness of life. For if we have been united with him in a death like his, we will certainly be united with him in a resurrection like his. We know that our old self was crucified with him so that the body of sin might be destroyed, and we might no longer be enslaved to sin. For whoever has died is freed from sin. But if we have died with Christ, we believe that we will also live with him. We know that Christ, being raised from the dead, will never die again; death no longer has dominion over him. The death he died, he

died to sin, once for all; but the life he lives, he lives to God. So you also must consider yourselves dead to sin and alive to God in Christ Jesus. (Romans 6:1–11)

## Song

Love's redeeming work is done;
fought the fight, the battle won:
lo, our sun's eclipse is o'er!
Lo, he sets in blood no more!

Vain the stone, the watch, the seal!
Christ has burst the gates of hell;
death in vain forbids his rise;
Christ has opened Paradise.

Lives again our glorious King;
where, O death, is now thy sting?
Dying once, he all doth save;
where thy victory, O grave?

Soar we now where Christ has led,
following our exalted head;
made like him, like him we rise;
ours the cross, the grave, the skies.

Hail the Lord of earth and heaven!
Praise to thee by both be given:
thee we greet triumphant now;
hail, the resurrection thou!

Charles Wesley, 1707–88

## Prayer

Lord Jesus Christ, in whom our redemption is made secure, we pray tonight for our world. Look upon us with compassion; visit our needs; save us now, Amen.